Daniel J. Hunter

A Sketch of Chili

Expressly prepared for the use of emigrants, from the United States and Europe to

that country, with a map, and several papers relating to the present war between

that country and Spain, and the position assumed by the United State

Daniel J. Hunter

A Sketch of Chili

Expressly prepared for the use of emigrants, from the United States and Europe to that country, with a map, and several papers relating to the present war between that country and Spain, and the position assumed by the United State

ISBN/EAN: 9783337245986

Printed in Europe, USA, Canada, Australia, Japan

Cover: Foto ©Suzi / pixelio.de

More available books at **www.hansebooks.com**

A SKETCH OF CHILI,

EXPRESSLY PREPARED FOR

THE USE OF EMIGRANTS,

FROM THE

UNITED STATES AND EUROPE

TO THAT COUNTRY,

WITH A MAP

AND SEVERAL PAPERS RELATING TO THE PRESENT WAR BE-
TWEEN THAT COUNTRY AND SPAIN, AND THE POSITION
ASSUMED BY THE UNITED STATES THEREIN.

BY DANIEL J. HUNTER.

NEW YORK:
PRINTED BY S. HALLET, No. 60 FULTON STREET.
1866.

CONTENTS.

FIRST PART.

SECOND PART.

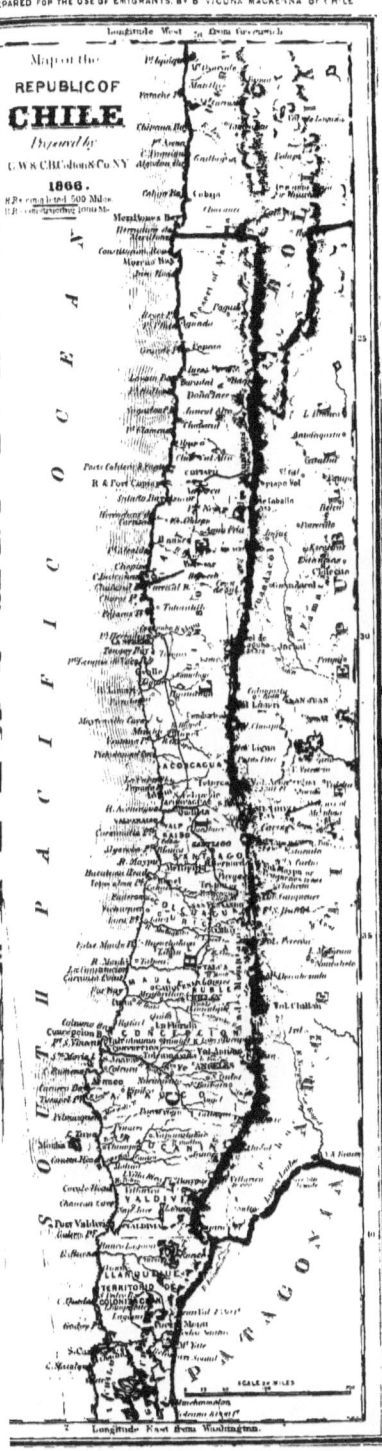

PREFACE.

THE present little work comprises two parts under separate titles. The first contains a physical description of Chili with statistical data up to the present time. The second relates to the actual war between that country and Spain.

Although in the last part of this pamphlet some idea of Chili is given to the general reader, we deem it important to go still further into details, in order that a country so admirably fitted to benefit emigrants may be better known.

For this purpose we give, in this preliminary part of our little work, a more minute description of Chili, paying particular attention to its geography, climate, agriculture and mines, and especially to the various laws, privileges and colonies which have been established in that generous and well-governed country, in order to favor the introduction of emigrants from all nations and of all religious creeds.

The lecture upon Chili, which we publish in the second part, given at the Travelers' Club, by Mr. Vicuña Mackenna, was of a pictorial, rather than a statistical and positive character. Consequently, we shall endeavor to supply that deficiency, but in such a way that one part will complete the other, without useless repetition.

With these few explanations, we have tried to condense, into a few pages, such important information as would make of this little pamphlet a real *vade mecum* or easy guide for emigrants.

POSITION AND LIMITS OF CHILI.

CHILI lies west of the Andes, and between the parallels of lat. 23° and 55° 59′ S., having a coast line of about 2,270 m., and a breadth varying from 200 m. to 40 m. Its area is variously estimated by different geographers at 146,300 sq. m. (Lieut. Gilliss), 348,000 (Abbé Molina), 170,000 (Lieut. Strain), and 240,000 by German geographers. Chili is bounded N. by lat. 23° S., which separates it from Bolivia, E. by the Andes, which form the dividing line between it and the States of the Argentine Confederation, S. and W. by the Pacific Ocean. It includes in its territory all of Patagonia west of the Andes, as the Argentine Confederation does that portion lying east of those mountains.

POPULATION AND POLITICAL DIVISIONS.

According to the latest census, taken in the Republic on the 19th of April, 1865, Chili is divided into fifteen provinces, with a population of 1,814,218 inhabitants; but making the usual allowance of ten per cent. for the number omitted, the actual population cannot fall short of 2,000,000.

In this proportion the Indians are not included. Those belonging to independent tribes form a community of some 30,000 souls.

The emigrant settlement of Llanquihue, where 2,000 German agriculturists live in prosperity, and the military settlement of Magallanes, are included in the full amount of the population—the latter having only 195 settlers.

The names of the provinces of Chili (which will be seen plainly marked on the accompanying map), their capitals and the population of each, are shown in the following table:

Provinces.	Capitals.	Population of each Province.
Atacama	Copiapó	79,227
Coquimbo	La Serena	145,874
Aconcagua	San Felipe	124,050
Valparaiso	Valparaiso	142,200
Santiago	Santiago	339,218
Colchagua	San Fernando	142,456
Curicó	Curicó	90,589
Talca	Talca	100,574
Maule	Cauquenes	188,181
Ñuble	Chillan	123,598
Concepcion	Concepcion	146,041
Arauco	Los Anjeles	71,945
Valdivia	Valdivia	23,429
Llanquihue	Puerto Montt	37,619
Chiloé	Ancud	59,022
	Total	1,814,218

This census shows an increase in the population of 375,098 over that of 1854, and of 730,417 over that of 1843. In the course of nature, the population of Chili will double every twenty-five years; but the current of emigration which has commenced to flow into the country, and which will be much greater after the war with Spain is over, will undoubtedly make her one of the most populous Republics of South America.

CLIMATE.

The climate of Chili is one of the finest in the world. Being in the south temperate zone, its summer answers to our winter, December, January and February being the hottest months. During three months little or no rain falls, and the thermometer sometimes rises to 90° or 95° Fahrenheit; but the sea breeze at night cools the earth, and renders the temperature refreshing. The mean temperature of the winter months at Valparaiso is 54°,

at La Serena 54.8°, at Santiago 49°, at Valdivia 46.8°.
The highest temperature known at Santiago is 90°, the
lowest 47.5°. At Valparaiso, the highest mean point in
summer, in three years' observation, was 78°, the lowest
62°, and the annual mean 70.8°. At Coquimbo, the mean
summer temperature was 63.6°, and the entire range only
16.8°. At Concepcion, the mean summer temperature at
3 P.M. was 73.5°, the mean for the year about 56°. In
Valdivia, the mean summer temperature is 60°, that of
the year 55°. At Santiago, the average number of hours
during which rain fell in the year, during 26 years' observation, was 215½, or about nine days. Further south,
the quantity of rain is somewhat greater; the island of
Chiloé having a very moist climate. Toward the north, on
the contrary, the rain diminishes in quantity, and on the
desert of Atacama seldom or never falls. As a result of
this equable and uniform climate, trees, fruits and flowers
of both tropical and temperate regions flourish well. In
some parts of the country the deciduous trees seem to forget to disrobe themselves. "The native palm and pine
of Araucania," says Lieut. Gilliss, "the chirimoya of tropical America and the medlar of Japan, the magnolia of
Florida and the olive of Asia, may all be found within
the compass of a garden, not less luxuriant in their proportions and ever verdant foliage than under the climes
of their origin." The atmosphere is remarkably clear,
especially at night. Indeed, so great is its superiority in
this respect over that of the Cape of Good Hope, which
was selected by English astronomers for their observations,
that it is estimated that a 6½ inch achromatic at Santiago
is fully equal to a 12½ inch one at the Cape. The crescent
of Venus was more than once seen with the naked eye by
astronomical observers.

TOPOGRAPHY.

The surface of Chili is greatly diversified. Beside the
Andes, which form its Eastern border, and which, unless
we except Ecuador, maintain a higher mean of elevation
and shoot up into more lofty peaks here than in any other
part of their course, there are two other ranges, of less
elevation indeed, but occasionally rising nearly to the level
of perpetual snow, which traverse portions of the narrow

strip which intervenes between the Andes and the Pacific, commencing near the 33d parallel. The more easterly of these traverses the central portion of the republic, and is known as the *Cordillera Central;* it is broken only by the passage of rivers until it terminates on the Pacific, opposite the northern end of the island of Chiloé. The other, known as *la Cordillera de la Costa,* or the coast range, separating from the central near its origin, follows more nearly the line of the coast, throwing off spurs occasionally eastward; it is of lower elevation than the central range, and is in some parts arable. Beside these mountain chains, there are multitudes of isolated hills, rising from the valleys, and forming bold promontories on margins of river, lake, and ocean.

The principal valley of the country is that lying between the central chain and the Andes; but there are innumerable others, lying between the coast and the central ranges, or guarded by the outlying spurs of the Andes or the central chain. Of the mountains of Chili, a large proportion are now, or have been at some time, volcanic. How many possess this character cannot now be ascertained; but the streams of lava which score the sides of many which are now quiet, and the not infrequent eruption of the fiery flood, as well as the occasional emissions of smoke and flame from those still active, indicate that the volcanic character belongs to the greater part.

In the northern portion, the coast and central Cordilleras spread out into the elevated plateau known as the desert of Atacama, which rises rapidly from the coast to a height varying from 4,000 to 10,000 feet, and from the comparatively level surface of which shoot up mountain peaks of great elevation, and often volcanic. By a recent proposed convention with Bolivia, Chili relinquishes all claim to that part of the desert lying North of lat, 23° South, and in this portion of her territory the only very lofty peak known is the volcano of Llullaillaco, which Dr. Philippi states at not far from 21,000 feet high. Few, if any, of the active volcanoes of the western continent exceed this height.

Geographers enumerate eleven passes over the Andes, from Chili into the Argentine Confederation, one or two of which, however, rest on tradition; two others, though practicable, and indeed comparatively easy, are not used on account of the opposition of the Indian tribes in the vicinity; others still are objectionable because of their great length or their liability to obstruction by snow. Of the whole number, only two are capable of being used and made passable for wagons.

GEOLOGY.

The great belt of Chili, between the Andes and the coast, ranging from eighty to a hundred miles in width, is traversed, south of lat. 31°, by numerous longitudinal ridges, called the Cordilleras of the coast, which are granitic. Further north, these spurs are more irregular in their direction, and are covered in great part with barren sands showing no trace of vegetation. This northern portion is of importance for its valuable mines of ores, while a strip along the south coast from Concepcion to the island of Chiloé, contains the principal mines of bituminous coal worked in South America. The country between the Andes and the coast is particularly interesting to geologists for the evidences which it presents of several successive elevations, which it has experienced within modern times. Some of these are historical, as that of 1822, when the coast at Valparaiso, and for many leagues north and south of it, was uplifted about six feet. The bed of shells and sea pebbles which marked its former beach is now that distance above the reach of the highest tides; and a succession of similar collections of shells of species belonging to the coast, accompanying terraces found further inland, and at higher levels, indicate as many as five uplifts of this character, but of much greater height, the difference of level between two terraces being found one hundred and twenty feet, and between the next two one hundred and eighty-two feet. Around the bay of Coquimbo these terraces are very distinctly marked in the hills; and as they extend back into the country, they spread out into plains, upon which towns, like the beautiful La Serena, the capital of the province of Coquimbo, are built. Near Valparaiso, comminuted sea shells of living species are found at elevations of over five hundred and fifty feet; and some, it is stated, have been met with even one thousand three hundred feet above the sea level.

The most noted mineral springs are those of Apoquindo, Colina, Cauquenes, Panimávida, Cato, Soco, and Doña Ana; the principal constituents of which are chloride of calcium, chloride of sodium, chloride of magnesium, and sulphates of soda and lime, with occasional traces of iron and alumina. About seventy-five miles east south-east of Chillan are found hot sulphur springs, almost up to the line of perpetual snow on the Nevada de Chillan. They are much frequented, and are reputed to possess extraordinary medicinal virtues, particularly the last, for constitutional diseases and shattered nature.

HYDROGRAPHY.

The hydrographic system of Chili, although deficient and scarce in the north, owing to the dryness of the atmosphere and the comparative depression of the Andes, is very powerful and widely spread, particularly in the region of the south not yet explored. The lakes are numerous, but few of them are very large. With the exception of a few salt ponds or coves near the coast, they are bodies of fresh water, accumulated in the valleys high up in the central range of the Andes. The largest is Llanquihue, at the foot of the Andes, in the province of Valdivia; it is nearly triangular, thirty miles long, and twenty-two miles in its greatest width. Near it, and lying in the same plain, are Todos los Santos, or Esmeralda, so called on account of its green, transparent, and beautiful water, eighteen miles long and six miles wide, and Rupanco, twenty-four miles long and four miles broad. Puychué, a short distance north, is a trifle larger; and some ten or twelve miles further north is Ranco, a very irregular shaped lake, thirty-two miles long and eighteen broad. Immediately east of Valdivia are five small lakes, which form the head waters of the Valdivia river; near latitude 39° is Villa Rica or Llauquen, which covers more than one hundred square miles. In the province of Concepcion there are two lakes —Guilletué, with a surface of about fifty square miles, lying high up in the Andes, and La Laja, celebrated for its picturesque scenery, and for the beautiful fall, a miniature Niagara, at its outlet, a short distance below.— North of these there are no lakes deserving the name, but small bodies of water, the product of the melting snows drained into extinct craters, covering a surface of from three to twenty square miles, diversify the rugged scenery of the rough granite masses of the Andes.

The rivers of Chili are all of inconsiderable length, rising in the Andes, and finding their way by numerous waterfalls and rapids to the Pacific. When swollen by the melting of the mountain snows, they discharge large quantities of water, and no inconsiderable quantity of alluvium, gravel, and even the debris of rocks into the Pacific, and almost all of them have, in consequence, considerable bars at their mouths. The following are the principal rivers : The Biobio rises in an extinct volcano in the extreme east of the Andes, lat. 38° 15', and takes a general north-west direction, receiving three considerable affluents —the Laja, Duqueco, and Bergara—and after a course of nearly two hundred and twenty miles, discharges its waters into the Pacific, in latitude 36° 50'. Like the other rivers of the country, it has a sand bar at its mouth, which prevents vessels of any considerable draught of water from ascending it. Inside the bar there is water enough for large shipping. A canal has been projected from the bay of Talcahuano into the river above the bar to obviate this difficulty. The river is navigable as far as Nacimiento, nearly one hundred miles, and maintains a steamer, which plies regularly between Concepcion and Nacimiento. The Maule rises in the Andes, in latitude 35° 10' south, and has a nearly due west course of about one hundred and fifty miles; it is navigable for small craft about seventy miles. The Valdivia rises in Lake Guanegué, in latitude 39° 45', and has a west south-west course; its length is about one hundred miles, and it is navigable for fifty miles. The Imperial rises in the Andes by several sources, in the vicinity of the parallel of 38° 30'; its course is south-west and west; its length about one hundred and fifty miles, of which about thirty are navigable. The Tolten rises in Lake Villa Rica, lat. 30° 5' south; its course is nearly due west; its length is about sixty miles; it is navigable, but not navigated, on account of the barbarous Indians on its banks. The Bueno flows from two principal sources, in two lakes of the Andes, lat. 40° 50' and 40° 40'; it has a course of about one hundred and ten miles, of which twenty are navigable. The other considerable streams, none of which, however, are navigable, are the Maypu, the Rapel, the Itata, the Aconcagua, the Mataquito, the Limari, the Coquimbo, the Huasco, and the Copiapó. The last, though at times a considerable stream, is often dry in summer.

COAST AND ISLANDS.

There are but few good harbors on the coast of Chili, though in the multitude of its small bays and indentations there are several roadsteads where, in fair weather, vessels may lie at anchor in safety. The best harbor is that of Talcahuano, in the bay of the same name, which is well protected, and with ample depth of water and room sufficient for the accommodation of the largest fleet. Coquimbo is the next harbor in point of safety. It is well sheltered on the west, south, and east, and as there are no tempestuous winds from the north, it is sufficiently secure. Close by it is a small land-locked harbor, Port Herradura, well adapted for repairing ships.

The harbor of Valparaiso is the most important on the Chilian coast, in the extent of its commerce, though, from its openness to northerly winds and the peculiar form of the bay, accidents to shipping are not uncommon. Caldera, in the bay of the same name, from which the largest exports from the silver and copper mines are shipped; Constitucion, within the mouth of the river Maule, an indifferent harbor, owing to the bar of the river at its entrance, but opening into a fertile region; Valdivia, an excellent harbor for small vessels; and San Carlos, on the island of Chiloé, lat. 41° 51', are the other principal harbors on the coast.

Before the pending war with Spain, Chili had only *nine* ports open to direct foreign trade, but now she has *fifty-five*. The Spaniards have consequently done a great service to the world. They have, it may be said, *discovered* with their big ships no less than fifty new ports unknown before to geographers and merchants.

The ports which were known before the war are the following: Caldera, Coquimbo, Huasco, Valparaiso, Constitucion, Tomé, Talcahuano, Coronel, Valdivia and Ancud.

The remaining forty-five now thrown open to the world, free of all custom house duties, are Chacao, Castro, Melipulli,

Calbuco, Rio Bueno, Carampangue, Lebu, Colcura, Lota, Lotilla, Penco, Lirquen, Curanipe, Buchupureo, Llico, Tuman, San Antonio, San Antonio de las Bodegas, Algarrobo, San José, Zapallar, Papudo, Pichidangui, Los Vilos, Tongoi, Guayacan, Totoralillo, Huanta, Carrizal Bajo, Sarco, Peña Blanca, Flamenco, Chañaral de las Animas, Paposo, Tartal, Cobre, Pan de Azúcar, Obispito, Dichato, San Vicente, Quinteros, Copiapó, Pajonal, Totoral, San Lorenzo.

The islands appertaining to Chili are numerous. The most important, and indeed the only ones of much intrinsic value to the republic are those of Chiloé and its archipelago. Possessed of a healthy though moist climate, a soil of extraordinary fertility, and with no elevation above 2,600 feet, a temperature in which ice does not form, and frost and snow are exceedingly rare, Chiloé may well be called the garden of the Pacific. It yields fine crops of wheat, barley, and potatoes every year, and the domestic animals propagate rapidly, and contribute largely to the commerce of the island. The potato is indigenous here, and by cultivation has reached a high degree of excellence. The inhabitants are amiable and hospitable, but, owing in part, probably, to the beneficence of nature in providing them a support with but little labor, they are inclined to indolence. The principal islands of the archipelago are San Pedro, Lilchuapu, Caylin, Tanqui, Lemuy, Quehuy, &c., &c. There are in all more than one hundred of these islands, of which twenty are settled, and have good harbors. These all abound in seals, otters, and shell-fish, and are well supplied with wood and water. Southward of these are the Guaytecas group and Huafo, similar in their general character. On the coast above Chiloé are several smaller islands, the principal of which are Mocha, lat. 38° 23'; Santa Maria, lat. 37° 3'; and Quiriquina, in the mouth of Concepcion Bay.

The most renowned of all the Chilian islands is the group rendered immortal in connection with De Foe's "Robinson Crusoe," Juan Fernandez. Aside from the fictitious interest thus bestowed upon them, these inconsiderable islands (for there are two principal and several smaller ones) have played a conspicuous part in the history of the South Pacific. First discovered by Juan Fernandez, in 1563,, they were abandoned in a short time by the colonists, who left their goats and fruit trees. Subsequently, they became a favorite resort for pirates and buccaneers, and afforded to Lord Anson for three months, a refuge where his crew might recover from the scurvy, and his vessels be refitted. They were visited by Ulloa in 1741, and in 1751 an attempt was again made for their colonization by the Spanish. Government An attempt twice repeated during the present century by the Chilian republic has not been quite successful.

BOTANY AND ZOOLOGY.

The vegetable and animal kingdom of Chili present a singular contrast, the latter being very deficient. There are, consequently, no magnificent wild beasts in the country. No lions, tigers, leopards; neither the small, ferocious reptiles which are the curse of most South American countries. It has been observed that Chili, being the healthiest country in the South, is precisely the one which produces most medicinal plants, and, at the same time, is free of all venomous animals or reptiles.

The potato is an aboriginal of Chili, as well as a very delicious kind of bean, called by the aborigines *porotos*, and a great many kinds of sago roots are found wild, particularly on the banks of the Biobio. A very sweet kind of juice called *chuño* is made out of this fruit.

Many of the forest trees are of great value for building and ornamental purposes. The araucaria, a species of pine, the alerce, a cypress, with a dark rich heart-wood, the roble, tiqui, mañu, muermo, and mayten are all valuable and durable woods. The coligue, a species of bamboo, is in very considerable demand for thatching roofs.

The animals of Chili are not as numerous as those of the countries east of the Andes. The mammals are comparatively few. M. Gay, an eminent French naturalist, enumerates seven species of *cheiroptera*, mostly of the bat tribe; twelve species of *carnivora*, embracing four of the cat tribe, three foxes, one weasel, two polecats, the nutria and the otter; six species of the *phocidæ*, embracing the seal and his congeners; one marsupial, the *didelphys elegans*, peculiar to Chili: twelve genera and twenty-five species of rodents, of which twelve belong to the mouse family; the chinchilla and its congeners, and the cavy or mountain rabbit. There are only two species of the *edentata*, the dasypus and pichiciego, the latter a very rare animal, found only in Chili. There are three ruminants, the guanaco, the largest of the llama tribe, and two of the deer tribe, the pudu and the huemul. There are four species of *cetacea*, two dolphins, the sperm whale, and the right whale. There are eleven species of *reptilia*, five of which are saurians, four ophidians, one frog, and one toad. The birds are more numerous. The *raptores*, embracing the condor, the vultures, hawks, and owls, are largely represented. The great order of *incessores* has numerous representatives of its every tribe and family, many of them of superb plumage, and some of wonderful powers of song. The dove and pigeon tribes are also found in considerable numbers, and the waders (*grallatores*) and swimmers (*natatores*) are almost numberless, several of the species being peculiar to the western coast of South America.

Among the fishes, we find three species of the perch tribe, all new; one of the *atherinidæ*, the kingfish; three of the *siluridæ*, one a new genus and species; two *clupidæ* both new, one a new species of the shad; one *cheirodon*, a new genus of the *characini* family, and a new myxinoid, having an affinity with the lamprey eel of our northern waters. Crustaceans and mollusks are abundant, especially in Chiloé and the other southern provinces, but have not been very fully examined. The *choros*, a peculiar species of oyster, exists in great quantities along the coast, and forms a favorite dish with the inhabitants, particularly those of the Quiriquina, in the bay of Talcahuano, which have really a delicious flavor.

HISTORY.

The history of Chili, as well as that of all the European colonies of North and South America, offers very little interest up to the time in which they shook off the bonds of their mother countries.

Of aboriginal Chili little is known. Prior to 1450, the present territory was inhabited by the ancestors of the Indian tribes no longer to be found there, who seem to have all descended from a common stock, and called themselves by the general title of Mapu-che, people or children of the land. They were subdivided into a number of tribes, but all spoke a common language. In 1450, the reigning Inca of Perú, Yupanqui, formed the project of extending his sway over the Chilian territory, and having stationed himself with a powerful army in Atacama, despatched his trusty lieutenant, Chinchiruca, with ten thousand men, southward to subdue the Mapu-che.— With that tact which characterised the policy of the Incas, Chinchiruca sought to win rather than conquer these rude and warlike tribes; and such were his powers of persuasion, that tribe after tribe yielded to the "children of the sun," and in six years' time the inhabitants of Northern Chili, for six hundred miles, from the Atacama frontier, paid fealty to the Peruvian monarch. But his sway was destined to receive a check. Pushing further south, his officers and soldiers encountered, on the further bank of the river Maule, a warlike tribe known as the Promaucaes, who returned a defiant answer to the summons and representations of the Inca, and refusing all overtures for peace, attacked the Peruvian troops. A desperate battle followed, lasting three days, in which both armies were too thoroughly shattered to renew the conflict. Upon hearing of the result of this battle, Yupanqui wisely resolved to forbear offensive warfare, and to maintain only what he already possessed.

When some eighty years later, the Spaniards had overthrown the empire of the Incas, they found Chili owning a nominal allegiance to the Peruvian monarch, and resolved to subjugate that country also ; and Diego Almagro, from the double motive of glory and gold, led an expedition across the mountain passes of the Andes. When he reached Copiapó, one-fourth of his Spanish troops and two-thirds of his Indian allies had perished from cold, fatigue and starvation. They were received by the people very kindly, and met no opposition till they reached the territory of the Promaucaes, where, like their predecessors, they found a foe so brave that they were fain to pause and retrace their steps.

Almagro and the remainder of his force returned slowly and sadly to Perú, and five years elapsed ere another expedition to Chili was attempted. Pedro Valdivia, a prudent and able commander, was selected for this service, and so well did he arrange his plans that, though occasionally meeting with hostile bands of Indians, he penetrated, without serious difficulty, to the river Mapocho, and encamped upon the present site of Santiago. Finding the location pleasant and the adjacent country fertile, he here founded a city, to which he gave the name of the patron saint of Spain.

Scarcely had he fortified himself in his new town, however, before the Indians, availing themselves of his temporary absence, assailed it, and would have taken it but for the hasty return of the commander; but though balked of their intended prey, they returned again and again to the charge, till Valdivia was compelled to send for re-enforcements from Perú. After the arrival of these he proceeded southward, and though the Promaucaes, the ancient foes of Almagro and of the Inca's forces, seem to have offered no effectual opposition to his progress, he found, after crossing the Itata, which formed their southern boundary, a new foe, braver, fiercer, and readier for the fray than any he had hitherto encountered—the Araucanians, for the first time appearing on the page of history. So terrible and unexpected was their first attack, that it well nigh annihilated Valdivia's army, and compelled him to retreat to Santiago, and eventually to return to Perú for further re-enforcements.

He returned in 1550 with a large and well-appointed force, and founded the city of Concepcion, on a site now known as Penco. Here the Araucanians rallied their forces, and with four thousand men under Caupolican, atacked the new city, and with a more determined valor than any Spanish general had before witnessed, resisted the skill and bravery of the Spanish troops. It was not until the fall of their leader that they would yield an inch of ground. Conflict after conflict followed. The Indians, after a time, were led by a young Auraucanian captive named Lautaro, who had been reared in Valdivia's family, whose skill as a commander made him a formidable foe.

In 1553, Valdivia was captured by the Indians, and put to death. Emboldened by their success, the Indians destroyed Concepcion, resisted all attempts to rebuild it, and eventually marched upon Santiago, and placed it in great peril, but were finally repulsed, and the brave Lautaro fell.

During the next two hundred and fifty years, a protracted

war followed, the brave Araucanians never yielding the country to their hated invaders. This aboriginal love of independence has been ascribed as a natural reason of the powerful feeling shown afterward by the Chilians, heirs in some respect of those courageous men, in sustaining their honor and independence against all foreign people.

With the exception of the war with the Araucanians, in which many Governors of Chili lost their power and life, and which was terminated in the peace of Negrete, in 1793, there occurred nothing worthy of the notice of posterity during the dominion of the Spaniards. But in 1810, the energetic Chilians, feeling tired of being a mere appendix to the viceroyalty of Perú, which country they supplied with flour, hides, tallow, and other coarse articles and manufactures, rose against Spain, guided by the most powerful, influential and aristocratic families of the country. Among those who occupied the first rank was that of the Carrera, whose centre were the enterprising brothers, José Miguel, Juan José, and Luis, and that of the Larrain, called popularly the *family of the eight hundred,* owing to its vast relationships.

The Chilians fought two years bravely against the troops sent from Perú, but the two leading families of the country having unfortunately divided in feuds, the common enemy took advantage, and the army commanded by the Carrera being defeated in the battle of Rancagua, in the neighborhood of Santiago, on the 1st of October, 1814, the cause of their independence was temporarily lost.

But in 1817, the famous San Martin came to the rescue of Chili, traversing the Andes from the Argentine Republic with an army of four thousand men, and defeating the Spaniards twice in Chacabuco (February 12th, 1817), and on the plains of Maipo, in the outskirts of Santiago (the 5th of April, 1818), assured for ever the independence of the Republic.

General O'Higgins, a native of Chili, and son of the most distinguished vice-king of Perú, Don Ambrosio O'Higgins, an Irishman by birth, was appointed supreme chief of the Republic, as an honor paid to his bravery and patriotism, having been San Martin's most active lieutenant.

San Martin and O'Higgins, once in power, planned the

liberty of Perú, where the stronghold of the Spanish power lay, and in 1820, sent a naval and military expedition, the first under the famous Lord Cochrane, and the last guided by San Martin himself. After a successful and wonderful campaign, the Chilian army occupied Lima on the 21st of July, 1821, and a week afterwards the independence of Perú was solemnly proclaimed (28th of July, 1821).

After a glorious career, the military government of Gen. O'Higgins was superseded by that of Gen. Freire (Jan. 28, 1823). A decade of troubles abortive attempts at a unitarian and federal government, followed, until the country was pacified by the superior talent and energy of a civilian, Don Diego Portales, who, although a merchant by profession, showed the most extraordinary talents as a Statesman. Under a rather despotic Constitution the political factions were subdued, until the cords of power being too much stretched, Portales himself fell a victim to a military revolt, while organizing an expedition against the President of Bolivia, General Santa Cruz, who had usurped the supreme power of Perú.

The Expedition was carried out, notwithstanding the death of Portales (June 16th, 1836), first under General Blanco, and afterwards under the command of the successful General Búlnes, who completely defeated Santa Cruz in the famous battle of Jungay (January 20th, 1839), restoring thus for the second time to Perú its independence and liberty.

In 1841, General Búlnes was elected President, on his return from Perú, and governed quietly for two constitutional terms. In 1851 D. Manuel Montt, an eminent lawyer, was elected, and although he governed with a party rather than with the nation, he kept the power until, in 1861, Don José Joaquin Perez was elected President.

The first period of his administration ends next September, and it is very probable that he will be elected for the next term, owing to his good management of the public affairs, particularly in sustaining the honor of the country in the war with Spain.

This war is the great event of South America and Chili. We have referred to it more fully in the *second* part of this work, and we have only to say here that the Chilians commenced it gloriously, attacking and taking one of the Spanish ships-of-war, the "Covadanga," off the port of Papudo, on the 26th November, 1865.

By a treaty of alliance, Perú takes sides with Chili in the war with Spain, which was solemnly declared in Lima on the 15th January last. Ecuador followed on the 30th of January, and it is expected that Bolivia, New Granada and Venezuela will come forward to support the old and glorious brotherhood of the South American Republics.

This struggle cannot last long, as Spain has no power to carry it on, and all the nations of Europe are opposed to her shameful depredations upon the prosperous republics of South America.

GOVERNMENT.

The Republic of Chili is governed under the rule of a very strong political constitution, framed through the influence of the famous Portales, or at least of his party, and which was sanctioned on the 25th May, 1833. It is, consequently, the oldest constitution of America, after that of the United States, and it is must be acknowledged that its age is its principal title to respect.

The form of government is republican, representative and electoral, all citizens possessing certain political qualifications being electors and eligible. Most of the German emigrants, settled in the south of Chili, have a right to vote, and have taken a lively part in the politics of the country.

The three political branches of a representative government, the executive, the legislative and the judiciary, are clearly defined by the Constitution.

The President, or chief of the executive, is elected for five years, and is eligible for a second term, but not for a third, until a period of five years has elapsed. He is assisted by a Council of State, composed of thirteen persons, all of his own choosing, and removable at his will. There are four cabinet ministers, viz.—of foreign and home affairs, of finance, of war and marine, of justice, religion and education. They are responsible for every official act, and cannot leave the country for six months after the expiration of their term of public service. No order or document from the president is legal without the countersignature of the minister to whose department it belongs.

The Legislature is composed of a Senate of twenty members, elected for nine years, one-third of whom go out of office every three years, and a House of Deputies, consisting of one for every twenty thousand inhabitants, elected for three years. Government officers may be members of either branch of the legislature, and still hold their offices. They may, and often do, also, represent more than one constituency.

The judiciary consists of primary courts, three courts of appeal, and a supreme court. The judges of the higher courts are appointed for life, or rather during good behavior, and can only be removed by impeachment.

The Government of Chili has acquired great credit for the management of her relations with foreign powers.— This peculiar trait has been ascribed to the natural discreet and quiet character of the people, and in some measure to the interference and wisdom of the celebrated Venezuelan savant, Don Andres Bello, undoubtedly the most famous Spanish writer on international law, and chief clerk for many years of the foreign department.

During the last forty-seven years, Chili has ratified not less than twenty treaties with foreign nations. The following table shows the names and the date of those conventions :—

Treaties between the Republic of Chili and the Argentine Confederation,			Feb. 5, 1819 Aug. 30, 1855
Between Chili and Bolivia,	- -	Oct. 7, 1845
do.	do.	Cerdeña, - -	June 28, 1856
do.	do.	Ecuador, - -	June 26, 1855
do.	do.	Spain, - -	April 25, 1844
do.	do.	United States, -	May 16, 1832
do.	do.	France, - -	Sep. 15, 1846
do.	do.	Great Britain, -	Jan. 9, 1839
do.	do.	do., - -	May. 10, 1852
do.	do.	do., - -	Oct. 4, 1854
do.	do.	Mexico, - - -	Mar. 7, 1831
do.	do.	New Granada, -	Feb. 16, 1844
do.	do.	do., - -	Aug. 30, 1853
do.	do.	Perú, - - -	Jan. 20, 1835
do.	do.	do., - - -	Oct. 7, 1845
do.	do.	do., - - -	Sep. 12, 1848
do.	do.	do., - - -	Nov. 7, 1854
do.	do.	do., - - -	Feb. 9, 1856
do.	do.	do., - - -	Dec. 5, 1865

THE PUBLIC REVENUE.

The public revenue of Chili is comparatively small, taking into consideration the extent, wealth and population of the country. But the reason of this is highly creditable to the country, as there is not on the surface of the globe a people less taxed than that of Chili. If the taxes were only half of those established in the United States, or a third of those of England, the actual revenue of Chili would be almost double that now collected. Indeed, there is in Chili, properly speaking, but one general tax, and that is paid directly by the foreign commerce——the Custom House duties, which constitute two-thirds of the public revenue. The other third is derived principally from two branches—the tobacco monopoly, which produces a million; and a light, although unequal tax on real estate, which yields a little more than half a million. Urban real estate and capital are not taxed at all in Chili; and, owing to this unequal distribution of charges, there exists a strong movement to establish a single direct tax, taking as a basis the capital or the revenue.

The amount of the public revenue in 1863, including all its branches, is shown in the following table:

BRANCHES.	1863.
Customs, - - - - -	$4,259,533
Tobacco Taxes, - - - -	1,091,821
Agricultural Taxes, - - -	641,474
Taxes on Sales of Real Estate, -	214,023
Imposition on Capitals, - -	4,300
Patents, - - - - -	74,316
Timber, - - - - -	102,214
Post Office - - - - -	123,404
Mint, - - - - - -	4,254
Tolls, - - - - - -	30,196
Railroad between Santiago and Valparaiso, - - - -	112,154
Eventual Branches, - - -	42,365
Total in 1863, - - - -	$6,700,659
do. in 1862, - - - -	6,287,155
Increase in 1863, - - - -	413,504

The increase of the public revenue during the last forty years is demonstrated in the following proportion :

1833,	-	-	-	- $1,770,761
1843,	-	-	-	- 3,001,230
1853,	-	-	-	- 5,552,485
1863,	-	-	-	- 6,700,659

The revenue of the Custom Houses, which at the time of the breaking out of the Revolution of Independence, gave only a monthly yield of $12,000, is exhibited in its uninterrupted increase by the following data :

Years.	Net Product.	Proportion for each Inhabitant.
1833 - - -	$1,025,385 - - -	$1,01 per head.
1843 - -	1,735,432 - -	1,60 " "
1853 - - -	3,358,540 - - -	2,35 " "
1863 - -	4,259,534 - -	2,51 " "

Another of the sources of the public treasury is the Post Office. At the end of the last century, there were only three weekly services throughout the country, as there existed only a few passable roads. The postage on letters, too, was very heavy (25 cents for a common two-cent letter), and consequently the communication was very limited. But lately (1853), the new America system of cheap postage has been adopted, with considerable profit to the Department and great benefit to the people. In 1853, the number of letters received was 195,351, and the year after, when the reform was put in execution, it was nearly doubled—306,569 being the number of letters delivered and received in 1854.

The increase of the Post Office revenue since 1833 is shown in the following table:

Year.	Net Revenues.	Per Centage.
1833 - - - -	$20,525 - - -	$0,02 per head.
1843 - - - -	44,060 - - - -	0,04 " "
1853 - - - -	52,982 - - -	0,04 " "
1863 - - - -	123,404 - - - -	0,07 " "

There are now more than one hundred and fifty general and local post-office stations throughout the country, and theservice, except in the further provinces, is, in most cases, daily. The vast extent of coast navigation in Chili affords peculiar facilities for frequent communication between its several provinces and cities. Copiapó, the northernmost extremity of the Republic, is only 30 hours' steaming from Valparaiso, and Chiloé, the southern extremity, only double that time.

The foreign debt at the end of 1865 was $10,678,500, $3,575,000 of which was an old English loan of 1822, at 3 and 6 per cent., and $7,193,500, the loan of 1858, at 4½ per cent. But as the value of the railroad between Valparaiso and Santiago, and the shares held by the government in other railroads is represented by the amount of $15,778,108, itmay be said that Chili has no foreign debt, or, at least, that she can pay it at any moment and be free of all obligation to foreign capital.

COMMERCE.

The commerce of Chili with foreign nations, particularly with England, is very large. It is represented, indeed, as among the first commercial nations of the world. The natural productions are fitted for a wide exportation; the wealth of the inhabitants permits them to invest large sums in foreign and luxurious importations, and the fact of Valparaiso, the principal port of Chili, being a kind of depot for merchandise which comes around the Horn for the supply of the south of Bolivia (via Cobija) and the north-west provinces of the Argentine Republic—through the several passes of the Andes—accounts for the prodigious commercial transactions that take place there yearly. The liberality of the commercial laws conduce greatly to this result.

The amount of exportations from the country during the last four years (1861-'64) amounts to the extraordinary sum of $89,705,771, and the importations to $73,257,851, making a round sum of $162,963,622, according to the following statistics:

IMPORTATIONS.

In 1861,	-	-	-	-	-	$20,349,634
" 1862,		-	-	-	-	21,994,432
" 1863,	-	-	-	-	-	20,118,852
" 1864,		-	-	-	-	27,242,853
Total,		-	-	-	-	$89,705,771

EXPORTATIONS.

1861, - - - -	$16,676,314
1862, - - - - -	17,226,655
1863, - - - - -	20,487,517
1864, - - - -	18,867,365
Total, - - -	73,257,851

The principal articles exported in 1864 were the following:

Copper in bars, - - - -	$9,506,957
" regulus, - - - -	4,714,912
Wheat, Flour, - - - -	2,321,090
Silver in bars, - - -	1,638,272
Copper Ore, - - - -	1,268,588
Wheat, - - - -	1,039,071

The different countries to whose markets those productions were sent appear in the last statistical records in the following per centage:

England, - -	58.41	pr. ct. of total exportation.
Peru, - - -	13.93	" "
France, - -	11.19	" "
Australia, - -	3.59	" "
North America, -	2.98	" "
California, - -	1.96	" "
Germany, - -	1.63	" "

The principal articles of importation are marked thus for the same year (1864):

Plain cotton goods, - - - -	$970,387
Refined sugar, - - - - -	961,697
Cattle from Argentine Republic, - -	810,896
Calicoës, - - - - -	689,291
Ground sugar, white and brown, - -	647,591
Coal, - - - - - -	574,395
Yerva Mate, - - - - -	537,368

The countries from which the imports were sent are

England,	43.46	per cent.
France,	20.93	"
Germany,	9.11	"
Argentine Republic,	5.58	"
North America,	5.52	"
Peru,	3.99	"
Brazil,	3.92	"

The internal commerce by sea, and its wonderful increase, is shown by the following figures:

1861,	$16,696,921
1862,	23,919,972
1863,	25,003,789
1864,	28,896,783
Increase over 1863,	3,892,994
" 1862,	4,977,811
" 1861,	12,199,862

In the foregoing statistics, the *transit* commerce from Chili to Bolivia and the Argentine Republic, which amounts to several millions, is not included.

After the general but accurate review of the commerce carried on during the year before last, we subjoin some other minute statistics, which we deem of interest to the general reader, about the commercial wealth of Chili. In 1855 the imports were $25,988,925; in 1856, $29,804,041; and in 1857, $31,800,209. The exports of 1855 were, $19,110,589; in 1856, $18,159,522; and in 1857, $20,126,461. The following table particularizes the exports of the latter year:

Bars of gold and gold coin,	$497,736
Silver and silver ores,	4,725,655
Copper and copper ores,	10,760,589
Wheat,	1,050,718
Flour,	798,112
Biscuit, bread, &c.	108,223
Barley,	257,970
Beans,	24,904
Peas and maize,	4,835
Potatoes,	35,506
Wine and chicha,	1,612
Nuts and dried and fresh fruits,	89,052
Salt beef,	10,880

Charqui, or jerked beef,	- -	104,173
Butter and cheese,	- - -	36,055
Tallow and lard,	- - -	2,729
Hides, horns, and hoofs,	- -	501,104
Goat, sheep, and chinchilla skins,	-	40,861
Wool,	- - -	397,643
Assorted provisions,	- -	27,189
Dried fodder,	- - -	41,790
Cords, rope, and rigging,	- . -	18,464
Planks and lumber,	- - -	265,287
Coal,	- - - -	176,765
Guano,	- - - -	5,600
Miscellaneous,	- - -	143,009
Total,	- - -	$20,126,416

The principal imports are distilled spirits, ale and porter, alpaca goods, baizes, bedsteads, books, buttons, cabinet-ware, calicoes, candles, canvas, carpets, carriages, cassimeres, cigars, cloths, clothing, coal, cotton and woollen goods, crape shawls, drugs, earthen and glass ware, gloves, gold in bars and coin, gunpowder, horned cattle and horses, household furniture, indigo, iron and iron goods, jewelry and cutlery, leather, linen goods, machinery, matches, yerva mate, merino cloths, muslins, molasses, oils, paints, paper, perfumery, pianos, quicksilver, raisins, rice, rigging, salt, satin goods, shoes and boots, silks, silver coin and bars, soap, steel, straw goods, sugar, tea, tin, tobacco, umbrellas and parasols, velvets, watches, wax, wines, and wool shawls. The following table gives the quantities of sugar, coffee, tea, and iron imported from 1844 to 1855:

Years.			Sugar, arrobas.	Coffee, cwt.	Tea, lbs.	Iron, cwt.
1844,	-	-	245,217	1,939	26,713	38,600
1845,	-	-	330,307	1,722	31,552	52,963
1846,	-	-	607,427	1,941	25,227	18,991
1847,	-	-	511,837	921	33,728	14,968
1848,	-	-	413,956	2,064	49,568	32,989
1849,	-	-	227,097	1,447	53,032	43,956
1850,	-	-	508,281	2,737	36,513	58,969
1851,	-	-	850,729	1,670	80,447	38,842
1852,	-	-	730,757	4,188	104,207	115,835
1853,	-	-	711,635	3,069	65,895	14,176
1854,	-	-	731,427	2,954	89,960	52,859
1855,	-	-	1,513,815	4,518	112,264	155,740

The imports of sugar into Valparaiso from January 1 to August 15, 1858, were 336,926 *arrobas* of 125 pounds each, and the stock on hand at the latter period was 94,000 *arrobas*.

The exports to England were, in 1854, £1,380,563; in 1855, £1,925,271; and in 1856, £1,700,776. The imports of English produce were, in 1852, £1,167,494; in 1853, £1,264,942; in 1854, £1,421,855; in 1855, £1,330,385; and in 1856, £1,946,010 The imports of foreign and colonial produce from England were, in 1854, £43,589; in 1855, £56,688; and in 1856, £64,492. The English exports to Chile in the half-year ending June 30, 1858, were £602,956, showing a decrease of £120,492 compared with the same period of 1857. The exports of Chili to France were $218,000 in 1851, $250,000 in 1852, $240,000 in 1853, $650,000 in 1854, and $980,000 in 1855. The imports from France were $4,800,000 in 1851, $3,550,000 in 1852, $4,400,000 in 1853, $4,000,000 in 1854, and $5,600,000 in 1855. The commercial intercourse of Chili with the United States has been very variable. In the earlier years of Californian emigration she sent large quantities of flour, grain, and lumber to that State, and took freely of our goods in return. Since that time her exports to this country have continued in large amount, but she receives little except money in return, the balances being mostly settled in Europe, where she is a debtor. The following table shows the amount of her commerce with the United States for several years:

	EXPORTS.		IMPORTS.
1849,	$3,589,888	1849,	$1,100,345
1850,	4,012,612	1850,	1,911,479
1851,	3,515,235	1851,	4,594,211
1852,	2,062,160	1852,	2,048,836
1853,	2,214,153	1853,	2,157,320
1856,	2,467,819	1856,	276,389
1857,	3,742,349	1857,	433,957

The following table of a more recent date shows how little the commercial intercourse between Chili and the United States has increased, or, rather, how greatly it has diminished since the late civil war in this country:

FOREIGN IMPORTS IN 1864 AND 1865.

	1864.	1865.	Imports from the U. S.
Rice	$103,159	$ 41,781	464
Sugar, raw, white and brown	644,027	614.564	1,652
Sugar, refined	958,746	1,312,026	184,904
Coal	84,695	156,802	240
Kerseymere	311,452	304,053	236
Beer	135,316	132,865	None.
Cotton drilling	394,786	388,540	—
White shirtings	966,833	1,021,397	—
Mixed goods	444,203	395,124	—
Bagging stuffs	335,686	339,474	—
Woollen shawls	283,139	107,826	—
Cloths.	177,811	182,941	—
Prints	688,767	599,693	—
Ready made clothing	232,813	161,159	—
Empty bags	253,967	236,364	—
Straw hats	173,419	143,640	—
Cottons	419,276	394,329	—
Paraguay tea	535,177	343,459	—

"If our merchants," said the able newspaper, already referred to, commenting on these extraordinary figures, "let this growing trade of Chili rest in English hands, they will show themselves less wise and less enterprising than they are reputed to be. There is no reason, with our ports on the Pacific side, why we should not do almost the whole of the carrying trade of Chili ; and certainly we ought, in the next two or three years, to quadruple our commerce with that country, which is, as we have already shown, one of the most thriving in South America."

It is a very singular fact, that the blockade of Chili, in the last four months of 1865, far from lessening the exportation of the products of the country, has increased them to a wonderful extent, as shown by the following statistics which one of the leading papers of New York (the "Evening Post," of February 27) has lately published, with an appropriate commentary upon the immense quantity of provisions furnished by the fertility of Chili to the markets of the world:

	1864.—*Kilos.*	1865.—*Kilos.*
Barley.	15,462,293	20,728 743
Jerked beef	313,778	484,213
Beans	735,219	2,348,208
Indian corn	162,791	2,371,242
Flour	24,164,638	36,878,041
Wheat	52,16,124	13,763,316

To complete this review of the commerce of Chili, we have only to add that the mercantile navy comprised several hundred ships, which, immediately after the war broke out, temporarily changed their flag, to resume in proper time their nationality. From the report of the Secretary of State in the marine department, presented to the Chilian Congress August 4, 1858, it appears that the mercantile navy of Chili, which in 1848 consisted of only 105 vessels, tonnage, 12,628, numbers at present 269 vessels, tonnage 62,209; showing an increase in ten years of 164 vessels, and of 49,581 tons. The coast trade of the Chilian flag exclusively presents the progressive increase shown in the following table:

Years.				Vessels.	Tonnage.
1853,	-	-	-	109	20,247
1854,	-			115	21,116
1855,	-	,	-	153	29,694
1856,	-	-	-	166	35,077
1857,	-	-	-	180	37,985
1858,	-			196	40,402

In the province of Chiloé 1,958 small vessels were (August 4, 1858) employed in domestic traffic, with a crew of 9,000 men.

The following table shows the navigation of Chili in 1857 :

Ports.	No. of Vessels entered.	Tonnage.	No. of Vessels sailed.	Tonnage.
Caldera, - -	—	—	—	—
Huasco, -	—	—	—	—
Coquimbo, -	292	86,732	309	94,665
Herradura, -	204	49,909	198	48,615
Papudo, - -	—	—	—	—
Valparaiso, -	1,117	351,836	1,093	335,436
Tuman and Llico,	—	—	—	—

Ports.	No. of Vessels entered.	Tonnage.	No. of Vessels sailed.	Tonnage.
Constitucion, -	184	31,151	188	31,337
Curanipe, -	13	1,092	13	1,052
Talcahuano, -	273	83,196	287	83,974
Tomé, -	180	44,366	180	44,376
Penco, - -	33	7,310	33	7,310
Lirquen, -	13	2,547	13	2,547
Coronel, - -	114	30,511	102	40,718
Lota, -	133	39,594	135	40,375
Corral, - -	96	27,101	94	26,244
Ancud, -	137	41,986	140	42,873
	2,789	797,341	2,785	799,542
To which should be added for other ports, say, -	125	40,000	120	37,000
Total, -	2,914	837,341	2,905	836,542

Finally, the number of vessels which entered and sailed from the ports of Chili in 1864, and their tonnage, is shown by the following figures:

Entered,	2830	vessels, with	1,011,702	tons.
Sailed,	2811	" "	994,184	"
Total,	5641		2,005,886	

PROGRESS OF STEAM NAVIGATION.

In the good old times of the Spaniards, when Chili was to America, more or less, what Spain is now to Europe, there was only a yearly direct communication with the mother country, when *el cajon del Rey*, (*the King's box*) was received with due ceremony, containing a few hundreds of letters from merchants or relatives abroad. To-day a single Company on the coast of Chili possesses no less than eighteen splendid steamers, with an aggregate tonnage of quite as many thousands. We do not believe, indeed, that there is in Europe or the United States a company possessing so large a number of ships, except, perhaps, that of the *Messageries Imperiales* in the Mediterranean.

The first attempt to introduce steam navigation in Chili was made, in 1835, by the well-known and enterprising Mr. Wheelwright, an American citizen from Newburyport, R. I. Mr. Wheelwright was to establish a line of two small steamers, of three hundred tons each, under certain conditions. But it was not until 1840 that he was able to carry out his enterprise, establishing a northerly communication between Valparaiso and Panamá with two little steamers built in England, the *Chili* and the *Perú* That was the humble beginning of the now prosperous and gigantic *Pacific Steam Navigation Company.*

It is a rather singular fact that this enterprise, having originated in an American merchant, has been developed entirely through English capital and English skill, to the continued exclusion of American interest, which says but little in favor of the energy and clearsightedness of the great *Commodores* of the United States.

The first voyage of the English steamers between Valparaiso and Panamá took place, to the great delight of the inhabitants along the whole Pacific coast, in October, 1840. Eight years afterwards (January, 1847), four steamers commenced to run between those two and the intermediate ports, and later, (in May, 1860,) a weekly communication was established between Valparaiso and Callao, touching at the following ports:—Tongoy, Coquimbo, Huasco, Carrizal, Caldera, Chañaral and Taltal, in Chili ; Cobija and Tocopilla in Bolivia ; Yquique, Mejillones, Pisagua, Arica, Ylo, Islay, Quilca, Chala, Pisco and the Chincha Islands in Perú.

At the same time the flourishing Company succeeded in establishing a new line of steamers from Valparaiso, southward, as far as Valdivia (1853), and afterwards to Puerto Montt (1858), receiving a subsidy of $40,000 yearly from the Chilian Government, as a liberal or rather prodigal encouragement for that remunerative service.

The Company now receives a heavy subsidy from th English Government; the post-office of Chili pays a fixed sum of $16,800 yearly for the carrying of the mails, without taking into consideration a fixed postage paid to the Company on the letters; and besides all these advantages, it possesses another and greater, viz.: a monopoly—its managers having had the foresight and wisdom to buy off all rival enterprises, particularly those attempted on a small scale between the United States and Chili.

The Pacific Steam Navigation Company deserves much credit for the skill, energy and liberality with which it has been kept up and improved. But the commerce of Chile and Peru has always looked with anxiety for the benefits of competition, principally from the American side, and there has always existed an unheeded but just complaint, on the part of South American travelers, that no attention is paid to their peculiar habits and tastes, everything on board the steamers—the food, hours for meals, night regulations, and above all, the independent brusqueness of the petty officers—being those of the most stringent old English style, so that it often happens that there are fifty or a hundred Chilian or Peruvian passengers who are obliged to fare entirely in the English fashion, so little acceptable to meridional palates, while there are few or perhaps no English on board.

In this respect there is, undoubtedly, great need of reform and improvement, but in every other, the English Company, for the capacity and quality of its vessels, the regularity and punctuality of the service, the professional merits of the commanders and officers, leaves nothing to be desired.

At present the Company possesses eighteen ships, and every year three or four new ones are launched in England and added to the line. The beautiful steamers *Santiago*, *Limeña*, and *Pacific*, are of 2,000 tons each, and were built in Liverpool in 1865. Of the balance, there are seven with a tonnage of from 1,000 to 1,800 tons, and eight with a varied tonnage of from 200 to 1,000 tons. The aggregate capacity of the fleet is 17,956 tons.

The number of passengers transported by this line in 1861, between Valparaiso and Panamá, was, 7,263, of which 1,997 were cabin passengers, and 5,266 steerage.

But this number, during the subsequent years, has been more than doubled, and of course the transportation of troops, which forms a heavy item of revenue, particularly in Perú, is not included in the above number. In 1860, the sum of $18,000 was paid by President Castillo for the transportation of a single battalion of infantry from Guayaquil to Callao. Lately, in 1865, a little steamer, belonging to the Company, was chartered on account of the Chilián Government, to carry the news of the sailing of the Spanish fleet from Callao to Chili, for $7,000. The *Paita*, the swiftest of the steamers on the line, was chartered from Callao to Paita, in November last, for the sum of $15,000, to carry important despatches, and performed that service in thirty hours, at an expense, perhaps, of two or three thousand dollars. Another steamer, the *Quito*, now the *Chalaco*, which cost the company from $250,000 to $300,000, was sold, after a good deal of service to the Peruvian Government for $600,000.

Another source of profit to the Company is the service of the mails.

The number of letters transported during the last five years (1859, 1863) shows, in a manner not at all flattering to the United States, how slight her intercourse with Chile has been as compared with that of other countries.

Years.	Europe.		U. States.
1859	28,961	letters	1,981
1860	31,429	"	2,136
1861	34,121	"	2,615
1862	39,948	"	2,780
1863	36,903	"	2,769

About the profits on freight, which yields by far the greater part of the revenue of the Company, there can be no perfect knowledge; but the profits must be enormous, particularly if we consider the large dividends paid to the shareholders, which, with a reticence worthy of the American system of keeping the public ignorant of all transactions for which the public nevertheless have to pay, are religiously kept secret.

Nevertheless, some idea of this extraordinary business may be had from the following facts :

In 1851, a few merchants of Valparaiso formed a Company under the name of *La Sociedad Anónima del Paquete del Maule*, with a capital of $74,000, for the purpose of running a little steamer between some of the intermediate ports of Chili south of Valparaiso.

The steamer *Paquete del Maule* made her first trip on the line about the middle of 1861, and eighteen months afterwards (December, 1862), the shareholders divided a profit of $11,000, after putting aside a reserve fund of $10,000. Six months afterwards (Jan. 30, 1863), a new dividend of $17,760 was paid, thus making, in little more than two years, a net profit of $38,760, or 32.38 per cent. of the capital.

Now, comparing the capital, the extent of the line, the priviliges, the subvention, and, above all, the *monopoly* of the English company, some faint idea may be arrived at of the splendid inducements offered by the South Pacific trade to the enterprizing capitalists of the United States, engaged in supporting rival lines on the north side of that ocean.

The Governments of Chili and Perú have always offered the most liberal terms to new companies for the establishing steam navigation in the Pacific. In 1853, Mr. Henry Griffin obtained the promise of a subvention of $60,000, during the term of ten years, for a line of steamers which was to make eight voyages annually between Valparaiso and Liverpool round Cape Horn, or rather through the staits of Magellans.

Lately (1865), the Chilian Congress sanctioned a law to appropriate $100,000 yearly to encourage another enterprize of the same kind, gotten up by French and English capitalists. But the war with Spain has put a temporary check to this important enterprise which will give new life to the prosperous English (not American) steam navigation companies in the Pacific.

The following table gives the tariff of passage by the Pacific Steam Navigation Company, together with the maritime distances between the several ports visited by its steamers. The average of the tariff per mile is 7 cents for passengers, $1.42 per ton for freight between Panamá and Valparaiso, according to the following table:

PACIFIC STEAM NAVIGATION COMPANY'S PASSAGE TARIFF.

Ports south of Valparaiso. From Valparaiso to	Distances in maritime miles.	Passage, 1st Class.
Tomé, . . .	240	$25
Talcahuano .	248	25
Lota y Coronel,	238	30
Corral, . . .	465	30
Ancud, . . .	603	55
Puerto-Montt,	663	60

PACIFIC STEAM NAVIGATION COMPANY'S PASSAGE TARIFF.

Ports north of Valparaiso. From Valparaiso to	Distances in maritime miles.	Passage. 1st Class.	Passage. 2d Class.	Steerage.	Freight per ton.
Tongoy, . .	175	$15	$12	$4	$6
Coquimbo, .	195	15	12	4	6
Huasco, . . .	293	18	15	5	6
Carrizal Bajo,	316	20	17	6	8
Caldera, . .	388	20	17	6	6
Chañaral . .	433	25	22	8	8
Taltal, . .	498	25	22	8	
Cobija, . .	676	55	50	15	10
Tocopilla, .	705	59	54	17	12
Iquique, . .	820	70	65	18	10 .
Pisagua, . .	856	70	65	20	12
Arica, . . .	926	70	65	20	10
Ilo, ...	1007	80	75	24	12
Islay, . . .	1067	80	75	24	10
Chala, . .	1209	85	80	25	12
Pisco, . . .	1400	90	85	26 .	12
Chinchas, .	1410	90	85	26	12
Callao, . .	1516	95	90	28	10
Payta, . .	2026	125	120	36	12 .
Guayaquil, .	2236	135	126	38	12
Panamá . .	3071	230	220	60	18

AGRICULTURE.

The agriculture of Chili forms the greater part of the wealth of the nation; and it not only maintains a robust people, who live cheaply and comfortably, but, owing to the low prices of food, affords facilities for working, at a small expense, mines that otherwise would not be productive. The immense exportation of mineral products depends chiefly upon the agricultural resources of the country, and at the same time yields from the exportation of its principal articles, viz., flour and wheat, an amount of several millions.

The husbandry of the country was not, up to within the last ten years, of the highest character. The soil of the arable portions is very fertile, and will yield, even of the cereals, from thirty to sixty fold; but, with the exception of a tolerably skilful system of irrigation, the farmers and planters were ignorant of improved methods of agriculture. Their ploughs were the rudest and most uncouth instruments imaginable, only scratching the earth to the depth of two or three inches; of subsoiling, the application of manures, underdraining, and the rotation of crops, they knew nothing; and the stubborn adherence of the *peons*, like that of ignorant laborers everywhere, to old methods, handed down from one generation to another, was a most effectual barrier to any considerable improvement. Still, with all these drawbacks, so fertile is the soil, and so much is it enriched by the detritus brought down by the mountain streams, that agriculture is a very profitable pursuit.

Lately, however, great improvements have been introduced, particularly by wealthy farmers who have visited Europe, and enterprising young men who have devoted themselves to the study of practical as well as scientific agriculture, both at home and abroad.

As far back as 1842, a normal agricultural college was established by the Government at Yungay, a suburb of Santiago, and has been carried on up to the present day, at an expense of nearly $130,000. Improved cattle, splendid breeds of horses, all kinds of foreign trees, shrubbery and grasses, agricultural implements of every description, and machinery, have been obtained by that useful institution, and have afterwards found their way to the large farms, the *chacras*, and the *quintas*.

Several manufacturers of agricultural implements, both in England and the United States, have sent their agents to Chili with successful results. The agent of the well-known Pitt's thrashing-machine succeeded in setting up thirty or forty steam engines in less than six months, in the latter part of 1858 ; and there is now in Valparaiso an American house (Rose, Innes & Co.) which makes a business of importing agricultural implements to the amount of several hundred thousand dollars yearly.

The farms are usually very large, frequently comprising several thousand acres, and herds of cattle, five, ten or twenty thousand in number, are pastured on the elevated plains and tended by the rough *huasos*, till the period for their slaughter arrives. The hacendados, or planters, usually reside in the cities, leaving their plantations under the care of mayordomos or overseers, and only visit them occasionally. The largest plantations in the country are those of La Compañia and Las Canteras, the latter with an area of over 200,000 acres. Smaller estates are called *chacras* and also *haciendas*, and the small farms are called *quinta*. The daily wages of laborers vary from twenty-five cents to thirty-seven cents, and in harvest time amount to fifty cents. In the northern part of the country, the people are far more industrious than in the southern region, where few laborers are to be found above the age of twenty-two. As soon as the young men marry in the southern provinces they yearn for independence, and live upon a little patch of land, which is generally presented to them by the planters. This class of laborers are attached to the plantation, and are called *inquilinos*. In return for this the land and accommodation granted to them, they are bound to assist the planter during the *rodeos* (cattle fair) and the *trillas* (threshing season).

A large part of the soil of Chili is uncultivated; but, when capable of tillage, is so fertile, and yields crops so abundant, that large quantities of cereals and meats are exported, as already seen, to Australia, Peru, England, and other countries. The two provinces of Atacama and Coquimbo, do not grow a sufficiency of grain or cattle for home consumption; but the other thirteen not only supply themselves and these, but exported in 1850 $2,693,545 worth of cereals, and in 1857 $2,242,354. The wheat crop of 1850 was estimated at 11,250,000 bushels; the number of horned cattle at 1,125,000, and 281,250 were slaughtered that year. *Charqui*, or beef dried in the sun, forms a considerable article of export, as well as of home consumption.— Santiago, Valparaiso, Concepcion, Ñuble, and Chiloé are the provinces which export the largest quantity of agricultural products. The principal grains grown are wheat, barley, oats, and maize; rye does well, but is not grown, because there is no demand for it. Beans are a very large and important crop, and peas are extensively cultivated. In the southern provinces, potatoes of excellent quality are raised. Ñuble, Concepcion, Valdivia, and Chiloé produce large quantities of timber and lumber.

According to the last agricultural statistics of the country, the quantity of *fanegas* of corn and vegetables produced (every *fanega* being equivalent to three bushels), was in 1862, as follows :—

	Fanegas.
Wheat,	3,161,722
Oats,	555,991
Maize,	212,989
Beans,	236,607
Lentils,	3,276
Peas,	56,524
Potatoes,	1,150,122

The quantity of liquors and wines produced by the famous vines of the several provinces in 1861, is estimated in the following figures by *arrobas*, a liquid measure equivalent to more or less than four quarts of the English system:

	Arrobas.
Chiloé,	5,632
Llanquihue,	26,633
Valdivia,	44,827
Arauco,	89,152
Concepcion,	301,926
Ñuble,	133,306
Maule,	163,858
Talca,	104,996
Colchagua,	194,689
Valparaiso,	64,132
Santiago,	292,309
Aconcagua,	162,586
Coquimbo,	50,422
Atacama,	12,245
Total,	1,656,703

The great diversity of climate, from the sunny and serene tropical valleys of the north to the moist hills of Concepcion, produces such a variety of grapes that all the famous wines of Europe can be easily manufactured, from the *lacrima christy*, which is made from the vineyards of Mount Etna in Sicily, to the light claret wines of Bordeaux, or the stronger red wine of Portugal. During the last ten years the manufacture of home wines has been introduced, and they are drunk by the inhabitants in preference even to the legitimate wines exported from the south of France. The laborers themselves will soon abandon the old, tasteless and unwholesome *chicha* for the common wine, which is being manufactured in large quantities in the neighbourhood of Santiago, and at a very low price.

MINES.

After agriculture, the great sources of the wealth of Chili, are its famous mines of gold, silver and copper. But having taken sufficient notice of their products in the second part of this pamphlet, we have now only to point out a few figures showing the locations and extensions of the principal mines.

In 1862, the principal mines worked in the several provinces were the following:

Provinces.	Gold.	Silver.	Copper.
Atacama, ...	...	247	994
Coquimbo, ...	18	34	338
Aconcagua, ...	8	9	228
Concepcion, ...	12		
Santiago, ...	·12	9	67
Valparaiso, ...	3	3	42
Colchagua, ...	7	3	21
Talca, ...	5		...
	55	305	1,710

The mines of the Cordilleras of the coast have proved productive, in the province of Santiago, of silver and gold. The latter metal is worked in veins associated with the sulphurets of lead, zinc, copper, and iron, four leagues from Rancagua, and is also collected in the deposits of the streams. The inaccessibility of the mining districts, and the presence of hostile Indians, check the working of the gold mines; so that the annual production of the whole country is not rated at more than $500,000. The silver mines, though once extensively worked, are now for the most part abandoned for the richer mines of Copiapó. This province likewise affords some cobalt and nickel, veins of the arsenical ores having been worked for several years near the mountain called Cerro del Volcan, and their products shipped to England. Copper mines are found along the course of the granitic and metamorphic rocks of the coast range and western spurs of the Andes from Santiago to the northern extremity of the country. This belt indeed abounds in metallic riches throughout its extent, even to Bolivia and Perú; but though lead, iron, bismuth, antimony, arsenic, zinc, and manganese are found, they are esteemed of no value, and the only mines worked are of the other metals named, and also to some extent of cinnabar. The importance of this ore is, however, greatly reduced by the cheap production of mercury in California.

Lately, discoveries of immense quantities of copper have been found in that part of the desert of Atacama which belongs to Chili. Several smelting establishments have been built by foreign mercantile houses, and principally by a very enterprising and respectable Chilian, Don José Antonio Moreno, who died lately in Santiago, leaving an immenes fortune, of which he made a very patriotic and liberal use.

The desert of Atacama, by its guano fields near Mejillones and elsewhere, and its inexhaustible veins of metals, will prove in future a source of revenue to Chile as abundant as that of her immense southern fields of bituminous coals.

COAL AND COAL FIELDS.

The coal beds of the province of Concepcion, were known as early as the year 1825. In 1834 they were examined by Mr. Wheelwright, Superintendent of the South Pacific Steam Navigation Company. In 1841 the formation was traced between Talcahuano and Valparaiso, and mines were soon after opened at the former locality. Coal has also been found in abundance near the mouth of the Laraqueto, and the beds are visible in the cliffs from vessels sailing along the coast. The most productive mines are in the districts of Coronel and Lota, the latter thirty miles south of the Biobio, in the province of Concepcion. About three thousand miners are employed, and the average annual produce is estimated at about seven hundred thousand tons, worth about seven dollars per ton. The coal beds are contained in strata supposed to be of the tertiary formation ; and though the coal of this age is never so good as that of the true coal measures, that of Chili is found to answer for steam and domestic purposes. Prof. W. R. Johnson examined some specimens said to be from the province of Arauco, which he describes in vol i. of the "Proceedings" of the Academy of Natural Sciences of Philadelphia, as of dull or pitchy black color, and nearly related in external appearance, to many of the richest bituminous coals, of America and Europe. By analysis they afforded 67.62 per cent. of carbon, showing a decided superiority over the ordinary brown coal of the tertiary. Reports of examinations of other coals of the region represent, however, a percentage of carbon not exceeding 40, and the presence of much iron pyrites. Coal is imported from England in large quantities for the use of steamers, and for smelting ores.

The largest coal works, managed by the most perfect English system, and established at an expense of nearly a million of dollars, belong to Mr. Luis Cousiño, who inherited them a few years ago from his worthy father, Don Matias Cousiño, a man who devoted his life and capital to the advancement of his country, and died in the prime of life. Mr. Cousiño, as well as Mr. Moreno and Mr. Urmeneta, (the wealthy proprietor of the copper mines of Tamaya), deserve the gratitude of their countrymen for their generous efforts to improve and develop the industry of the country.

RAILWAYS AND ROADS.

Chili is, perhaps, the South American country which presents the greatest difficulties for the making of good freighting roads and railways, and at the same time possesses the most of both. In 1862 there were not less than five railroads, comprising a distance of five hundred and forty-three kilometres, and three hundred and sixty-five broad roads, comprising fourteen thousand and thirty-one kilometres.

Lately, not less than five hundred miles of railways have been completed, and in order to connect the whole extent of the country, through the central valleys from Copiapó, southward to Concepcion, no less than one thousand miles are to be constructed, and already a part of this in process of construction, under scientific study and survey.

Having stated, in the latter part of this work, the location of the principal railroads, for which we refer the reader to the accompanying Map, we now proceed to give some interesting facts about the length, cost, progress and results of those enterprises.

The following table for 1863, shows the extent, in kilometres, of the railways in the country (1st column), the absolute cost in dollars of each (2d column), and the relative cost per kilometre (3d column):

	Kils.	Cost.	Cost per Kils.
From Valparaiso to Santiago,	183.98	10,834,798	59,020
From Santiago to San Fernando,	133.57	5,526,000	41,370
From Caldera to Pabellon	119.05	2,960,000	24,860
From Pabellon to Chañarcillo,	41.75	1,000,000	23,952
From Coquimbo to las Cardas,	64.61	1,040,000	16,000
	542.96	21,360,798	39,341

The number of passengers who traveled on the several lines in 1863, was 754,760, according to the annexed figures:

First class passengers,	124,436
Second " "	436,848
Third " "	193,476
	754,760

The produce of the several lines was $1,726,434, of which $615,076 were paid by passengers, and $1,111,358 for freight.

The whole extent of the lines of communication by land (taking into consideration only the cartable roads) and by rivers, amounted, in 1863, to 16,039 kilometres and were distributed in the several provinces, as shown in the following table:

Provinces.	Roads.	Rivers.	Railways.
Chiloé	———	37	———
Llanquihue	76	291	———
Valdivia	119	472	———
Arauco	2,190	452	———
Concepcion	1,434	171	———
Ñuble	388	152	———
Maule	550	99	———
Talca	777	94	———
Colchagua	1,636	———	51.50
Santiago,	2,680	———	145.88
Valparaiso	312	———	92.22
Aconcagua	161	———	27.98
Coquimbo	466	———	64.61
Atacama	3,242	———	160.80
Total	14,031	1,466	542.96

MANUFACTURES.

Chili has given but little attention to manufactures. The Government has, within a few years, endeavored to introduce them by offering exclusive privileges to manufacturers for a term of years, but with little success. Apart from the manufacture of common cloth, which, though woven in the rudest looms, possesses some qualities which the French and English goods have never been able to attain, and the coarser kinds of work in gold, silver, copper and iron, the very imperfect tanning of a small quantity of leather, and the simpler processes of the soap-boiler and candle-maker, the production of lumber, and the preservation of dried meats, there is little that can be called manufacturing in the country.

Nevertheless, there were, in 1863, no less than 132 steam engines, with an accumulated force of 9,970 horse power, equivalent to a force of 69,790 man power. Of those engines, 3 were employed in saw-mills, 13 in distilling liquors, 2 in blowing furnaces, 6 in flour mills, and 14 in coal mines. There is in Santiago a large manufactory of cloths in the French plan, and another of cotton goods in Valparaiso.

LATE PROGRESS OF CHILI.

Chili has ever been known as the steadiest, most prosperous and best governed of the South American countries. Although the revenue is not large, it is so economically and faithfully managed that all the branches of the public service are kept in perfect order. Public education, religious worship, the army, the navy, the public buildings, the roads, the preservation of harbors and lighthouses, the proper working of the mines, the protection afforded to manufactures, agriculture, and to public charities, the encouragement offered to emigration, the subsidies paid for internal or foreign steam navigation, and particularly the construction of telegraphic lines throughout the whole extent of the country, and of magnificent and costly railways, are attended to and paid for freely from the public funds or credit of the republic.

Slavery is prohibited by law, all traffic in it forbidden, and every person who treads the soil is declared free.

According to the report of the war department, presented to Congress, August 4, 1858, the standing army amounted to 2,193 men, being 463 less than the number required by law, and not including 469 pensioners and 48 military scholars. The officers of the army consist of 4 generals of division, 8 brigadier-generals, 6 colonels, 27 lieut.-colonels, 48 majors, 100 captains, 18 adjutants, 64 lieutenants, and 74 ensigns; total, 349. The existing police force amounted to 2,323 men, requiring for their support an annual expense of $461,449. An increase of 771 men, with an expense of $128,002 is proposed. The civic guard or militia consists of 40,466 men, viz.—682 artillery, 24,331 infantry, and 15,453 cavalry; the marine, of 2 corvettes, 3 brigantines, 1 frigate, and 1 war steamer, the whole mounting 71 cannon.

Lately, the differential duties on goods from the United States, Great Britain, Brazil, and other principal commercial countries, have been abolished. A new tariff was introduced May 8, 1851, and amended in 1865. Under Montt's administration, a civil code has been given to Chili, tribunals of commerce established, a discount and deposit bank founded in Valparaiso, and a bank to advance money on real estate, opened January 1, 1856.

The Mint of Santiago, which is considered the finest public building in South America, having cost upwards of a million of dollars, emitted in gold and silver coin, from January 1, 1850, to January 1, 1858, $18,103,877, comprising in this sum the recoinage of the old money excluded from circulation. In August, 1858, the amount emitted was about $61,000. To create a greater abundance of the circulating medium, a measure had been recently introduced into the legislature, authorizing the executive to purchase gold and silver bullion at the prices current in the market. A further relief in the money market was expected from another measure pending before Congress, authorizing Government to warrant the bills of the *Credito Hipotecario*, and to modify this institution. Efforts to promote the prosperity of the country are visible in every direction. The most prominent project before Congress was the establishment of towing steamers in the Straits of Magellan, and its accomplishment would bring Chili one thousand five hundred miles nearer to Europe, America, the West Indies, Brazil, and to almost all the other countries of the globe. Government has authorized the foundation of an anonymous society for mutual insurance against fire, under the name of the *Union Chilena*. The establishment of a Chilian Lloyd was contemplated, and a chamber of commerce was created at Valparaiso. Foreign skill is liberally used. Engineers and artillery instructors have been sent from France, and the metallic life boats of Francis from the United States. The merchants of Valparaiso proposed to devote $250,000 per annum to the establishment of steamers connecting that city with Monte Video and Buenos Ayres, and there was every probability of the realization of this project. Agriculture was beginning also to receive a fuller share of attention. In order to prevent the scarcity of breadstuffs, felt at the end of 1856, owing to an excess of exportation agricultural statistical offices were to be organised in the provinces, noticing beforehand the approximate consumption of grain in each locality, recording its annual production, so as to make it easy to take in time preventive measures to remove an extreme scarcity.

The construction of a powerful breakwater to protect the harbour of Valparaiso from the north winds, has been planned by order of the Government, and it is believed that it will be carried out at the expense of ten millions of dollars. The construction of another breakwater on the left bank of the river Cachapoal was proposed. New regulations for the sale of Indian lands in the State of Arauco had been brought forward, with the view of civilizing this State and of putting a stop to the collisions with the Indians on the frontier. Thus we find the utmost zeal prevailing to push on the progress of the country. Nor were charitable works neglected. Beside other institutions in various parts of the country, there were in Santiago forty-seven sisters of charity, intrusted with the management of the several establishments in that city, independently of a central home, wherein one hundred and fifty girls are educated. Four sisters of Providence were to take charge of of the Concepcion foundling hospital. In the Santiago lunatic asylum, ninety-six patients were accommodated in August, 1858.

Among the newspapers, we noticed the *Mercurio*, of Valparaiso, the oldest of South American papers; the *Patria*, of the same city, a remarkably well edited liberal paper; the *Independiente*, an able organ of the clergy in

Santiago and the *Ferrocarril*, undoubtedly the most influential and widely-circulated journal in South America. Almost every town has one or two papers, and the printing of books, particularly school books, is quite a flourishing trade. The first printing office was established in Chili in 1812, by an American of the name of Hœvel.

According to the able writer of the article "Chili," in the *New American Cyclopædia*, out of which much of this description has been extracted, suffering the necessary corrections, the Chilians "are more enterprising than the inhabitants of most of the South American States, aue the hacendados, or planters, and merchants often accumulate large amounts of property. With the exception of those destined for the learned professions, they have generally but little education. The men are usually robust, and although to the casual observer would appear wanting in muscular development, Lieut. Gilliss affirms that they possess much more strength than the men of other nations. He was more than once surprised by seeing men far from robust in appearance, take a load of 350 to 400 lbs., and trot off with it for half a mile without complaint. The women have fuller and rounder figures, and are generally pretty. They seem to have more intelligence and higher aspirations for intellectual culture than the rougher sex.°

EMIGRATION AND COLONIZATION.

Having given in this hasty sketch of the republic of Chili, the necessary facts and figures to make it sufficiently known to the general reader, there only remains

---

* We are sorry not to give a more minute account than that already offered in the historical sketch of Chili, of the famous Araucanian Indians, of whose ascendancy the people of Chili feel so justly proud.— They alone, of all the American tribes who came in contact with the Spanish or Portuguese invaders, have maintained their independence, notwithstanding a war of extermination was waged against them for a century and a half, in which all the appliances of civilization, all the bravery of the ablest commanders and the most experienced and veteran troops were brought to the work of their destruction. Aptly named the Ishmaelites of the new world, the best armies of Spain were powerless to drive them from their mountain fastnesses, or to subjugate them to the foreigners they hated. In this protracted contest, which ended in 1724 with the acknowledgment of their independence; the bravery, patriotism, and humanity of their leaders; the valor and devotion of the troops; the burning love of country, which led even the weaker sex to undergo the severest hardships to rid themselves of their foes, all constitute a heroic page of history.

for us the pleasanter task of addressing a few passing remarks to the class of emigrants for whose benefit this little work has been expressly prepared.

Among the many advantages offered by Chili to emigrants from all nations, is the mildness of the climate,
which makes its valleys some of the most delightful spots
in the world. This circumstance explains the fact, noticed by Humboldt and other travelers, that foreigners
once settled in that country even for a few months, always
show a great reluctance to leave it, and prefer it to their
own native lands.

Another powerful inducement to emigration has generally been the fertility of the soil, and its adaptation to
European agriculture. Emigrants to tropical or semi-
tropical countries in South America have found the climate
a great drawback to their settlement, advancement, and
even to their health. But in Chili, where the extraordinary
extent of the country affords every variety of temperature,
all the products, usages, and labors of Europe are met with,
and so readily, that new comers may consider themselves
at home after a few weeks' residence.

There is yet another peculiar advantage for foreigners
in the physical structure of the country. It is true that it
is the farthest land of South America, so far that a long sea
voyage intervenes; but, as a compensation rarely met with,
the emigrant, as soon as he finds himself on shore, is already
in the midst of the country, and needs not to make a long
land voyage, as is the case in the United States, Brazil, and
even on the Rio la Plata. There are no inland distances,
and consequently the inconvenience, expense, and fatigue of
traveling, as well as the expenses of settlement, are avoided.

The well-known hospitality of the people, is a virtue to which there is not a single traveler, no matter how
strongly prejudiced against Chili he may be in every other respect, who has not paid the warmest testimony. Those
dreadful diseases which afflict mankind, the yellow fever,
cholera, and other pestilences, are entirely unknown. The
general order of the public administration, the frankness of
the national character, and particularly the freedom of
conscience and the liberty and free exercise of all creeds,
which has been granted lately (July, 1865) by the laws of
the nation, are indeed strong inducements to emigrants
as the richness of the silver, gold, and wonderful copper
mines of that highly-gifted country.

Protestant churches were built in Valparaiso as far back as 1835. A respectable American merchant, G. G. Hobson, Esq., chief, at that time, of the well-known house of Alsop & Co., was the originator of that reform which has now assumed the character of a cherished institution of the country.*

But all has not yet been said on this matter. Notwithstanding so many natural reasons and interests to provoke a spontaneous current of emigration to that highly-favored country, the government has always endeavored to increase the settlement of emigrants and colonists by offering the most liberal inducements.

During the ignorant and hateful dominion of Spain, foreigners were looked upon with jealousy by the public authorities, and the laws interfered to prevent their permanent residence and even their visiting the country.

* A correspondent of the "New York Tribune" thus describes, under date of Jan. 15th, 1865, the inauguration of the first public Protestant Church in Santiago:

"The opening exercises were held the first Sabbath of the new year. The Rev. David Trumbull, from Valparaiso, preached the opening discourse from Rev. iii. 2—' Be watchful and strengthen the things which remain, that are ready to-day.' It was an able discourse, forcibly pronounced. The room was full: among others were seen the Hon. T. H. Nelson, our Minister, and the Hon. W. T. Thompson, the British Minister. This was a very gratifying feature, since it gave to the enterprise the influence of the representatives of the two most powerful Protestant nations. The press have generally made a kindly notice of the opening services, and not the least sign of dissatisfaction has yet been shown.

"The Protestants have come forward with great unanimity in their support. The first week all the pews were rented.

"The *Ferrocarril* of Santiago thus noticed this event:

'UNION CHAPEL. Last Sabbath took place the inauguration of the first Protestant Chapel in Santiago with the accustomed solemnities. Although, for some time past, the Protestants of Santiago have had a place for worshipping, yet it seemed that their growing necessities, and the ample protection of the present law for building churches and founding schools, demanded that they should enlarge their institutions, presenting them to the public, and not concealing them in some out of the way place. The new Chapel is sufficiently commodious, and is found in Calle Moneda No. 150, and is under the direction of the Rev. Mr. Gilbert. There were present at the ceremony some 200 persons among whom were found the Hon. T. H. Nelson, and the Hon. Wm. Taylor Thompson, the Captain and other officials of the British man-of-war Columbine, and many other English, Americans and Germans.'

"Invited by his co-religionists of Santiago, the Rev. Mr. Trumbull preached the opening sermon.

"This thing has not been done in a corner, and no opposition has manifested itself. It all speaks highly for the Chilians. They are becoming a liberal people, and for a long time they have had the credit of having had more illiberality than has really existed. But for the last three years public opinion has made great progress in the subject of religious liberty."

But since Chili has had a government of her own every effort has been made to procure for the country the benefits arising from the influx of sober, industrious, and enterprising emigrants. Since 1812 agents have been sent to Europe to promote emigration. Several societies have been formed with the purpose of lending aid to the emigrant, and lately (in 1853) the government appropriated, by a special act of Congress, nearly a million of acres, to be ceded to emigrants on the most liberal terms.

This territory lies in the southern part of Chili, surrounding the beautiful Lake Llanquihue, a large body of fresh water, which is navigated by many little crafts, and which will soon have the benefit of a regular line of steamers. The map accompanying this pamphlet shows the exact location of this happy and prosperous colony, under the name of the *Territory of Colonization*. But properly, the whole province of Llanquihue, the center of which is now occupied by the colony, may be considered a largefield allotted to European settlers.

The conditions of the settlement for emigrants cannot be more liberal, just, and generous. According to special act of Congress of August 28, 1858, the emigration lots are to be distributed under the following rules :

1st. Every head of a family will receive an arable lot of 48 acres (12 cuadras), and further, 24 acres for every male child which has reached the age of ten.

2d. The government defrays, at its own cost, the expense of landing the emigrants at the nearest port to the colony; keeps them for a few days on shore, and transports them to the place in which they will have their allotted land, and their cottages built by their own choice.

3d. A monthly pension of $15 is allowed to every family during the first year of settlement; and further, they receive the necessary seeds for the first season, a couple of oxen, a cow and calf, five hundred planks for building purposes, and one hundred pounds of nails. These articles are to be valued to the satisfaction of emigrants, and the amount is refundable by yearly installments, free of interest, and in very convenient proportions.

4th. Emigrants are exempted, during a term of fifteen years from all kinds of taxes, general or municipal, as well as from all kinds of public or civil service; and further, are entitled to all the rights of Chilian citizens, without any of the charges, by a simple declaration made in the presence of the local judge, that they wish to settle permanently in the country.

5th. The free exercise of religious worship is established, and every sect is permitted to have its churches, clergy, and schools.

The colony is governed by an *Intendente* appointed by the government, who at the same time acts as an emigration commissioner, and is empowered to decide all the difficulties arising out of the action of the emigration laws, having always in view the benefit of the settlers and the prosperity of the colony.

Under such liberal and judicious regulations the colony of Llanquihue could not but rapidly develop itself. Already no less than two thousand Germans are established within its precincts, and the treasury of Chili has laid out no less than two hundred thousand dollars for their settlement and comfort. It is true that the emigrants are bound to refund at least half of that sum; but proposals were lately presented to the government to bestow that amount upon the colony, and declare the settlers free of all obligations.

Agriculture and the cutting of timber and lumber, which is of a first-rate quality in those primeval woods, are the principal occupations of the community. In order to show the growth of the colony and the extraordinary fertility of the land, we here insert a table of the principal productions of the rural district of the settlement during the year 1861:

Articles.	Seed.		Result.
Potatoes, . . .	8,227	{ fanegas of 3 bushels. }	125,128
Wheat, . . .	1,815		19,844
Rye, ...	276		2,870
Barley and oats, .	572		8,726
Peas, . .	167		6,844
Maize, . . .	23		161
Beans, . . .	25		111

It is fair to say that such production has been doubled, or perhaps tripled, in the last five years, as there were in 1863 no less than forty-seven thousand acres under tillage.

The number of cattle at the same time was represented by the following official figures :

Cattle,	. . . .	34,205
Horses,	. . . . . .	2,574
Sheep,	. . . .	9,210
Mules,	. . . . . .	206
Goats,	. . . .	308
Pigs,	. . . . . .	3,214

The capital of the colony, called either Melipulli or Puerto-Montt, is situated on the large and beautiful bay of Reloncavi, opposite the island of Chiloé. It already has two hundred and twenty-nine houses, and two thousand one hundsed and fifty-two small cottages; there is a Protestant church and cemetery, with a chaplain paid by the community. The government maintains a public library, which is better attended than any other in the large cities of the country, and supports two or three free schools, in which the Catholic religion is not taught but to those children whose parents choose to educate them in that creed. Lately a plank-road has been completed for the exportation of the products of the colony between Melipulli and Lake Llanquihue, at an expense of $40,-000. It may be said that there is in Chili no public institution (and as such emigration is considered in that enlightened country) to which more attention is paid, or towards which more liberality and more kindness has been shown by the government during the last fifteen years, than in the *German colony of Llanquihue.*

Emigration, however, is not confined to that southern settlement, as foreigners of all nations, especially skillful workmen in practical arts and trades, find a ready and fair opening in all parts of the country; the miners in the north, the agriculturists in the central provinces, and the artisans, carpenters, bricklayers, blacksmiths, tailors, etc., in all the villages and larger towns. Lately some contracts have been made by proprietors of large farms engaging the services of emigrants for a certain number of years, allowing them a fixed salary and a considerable portion of irrigated land. But these enterprises have not proved quite successful, owing to the circumstance that the country does not want so many common laborers, but settlers of a higher grade.

It has been calculated that Chili, with the whole of her arable land under cultivation, is capable of maintaining a thriving population of not less than twelve millions of people. Now she supports only two millions, and of those but thirty thousand are foreigners. What a field there is open for the men who are brought out from the over-crowded countries of Europe to that distant but beautiful, genial, and prolific land, where everything is cheap, abundant, prosperous, increasing, and, above all, where there is the greatest blessing of mankind—LIBERTY!

CONCLUSION.

We deem it well to put into the hands of persons desirous of paying a visit to Chili, as a farewell ticket, the following directions:

The best way of reaching any of the ports of Chili, from Copiapó to Puerto Montt, is by the steamers plying thrice a month between New York and Aspinwall (six days), then crossing the isthmus by rail, taking on the other side the English steamers for the south, which connect at Panama with those of New York. The time spent in the voyage south to Callao, the principal port of Peru, is five days; to Copiapó, the most northern part of Chili, six days; to Valparaiso, three days; to Puerto Montt, three days—making twenty-seven days between New York and Valparaiso, including stoppages.

Fares from $150 to $400 through passage of first, second and third (steerage) class cabins.

And now God speed all who choose the happy land of Chili for their new home, and bless them with plenty, prosperity, and eternal happiness in the present and future world.

SECOND PART.

Part Three

CHILI

THE

UNITED STATES AND SPAIN;

A SERIES OF LECTURES, SPEECHES, EDITORIAL ARTICLES,
AND OTHER PUBLICATIONS, ON THE POSITION
ASSUMED BY THE REPUBLIC OF CHILI
IN THE PENDING WAR WITH
SPAIN,

CONSIDERED UNDER THE LIGHT OF THE

PRESENT FOREIGN POLICY OF THE UNITED STATES,

BY

DANIEL J. HUNTER.

NEW YORK:
PRINTED BY S. HALLET, No. 60 FULTON STREET.
1866.

PREFACE.

Several publications have been lately made in Washington and New York upon the actual war between Chili and Spain. But as most of these papers are official documents, interesting only to a limited number of readers, we have considered it useful, for the more general information of the people, both in the United States and in England, to reprint from the daily journals some pieces of a more popular character.

We have, consequently, given preference for this purpose, to the lectures and addresses delivered on several occasions by Mr. Vicuña Mackenna, a public writer of Chili, and to some of his essays published in that country, and which bear directly on the political intercourse maintained by that country with the United States.

In accordance with this idea, we publish in this pamphlet the following papers :

I. A lecture delivered by Mr. Vicuña Mackenna at the Traveler's Club of New York, on the night of the 2d December, 1865, on the "Present Condition and Prospects of Chili," which gives a general idea of this country so little known abroad, and introduces in the proper place the pending conflict with Spain.

II. A letter addressed by Mr. Vicuña Mackenna, in his private character as a citizen of Chili, to the Editor of the " Epoca," a leading journal of Madrid, and which was published, with some editorial comments, on the 2d December, 1865.

III. An address delivered by the same author at a public meeting in Panamá, held on the 9th of November last, and intended to explain the origin, character, and probable issue of that obnoxious question.

IV. The proceedings of a general mass meeting which took place in New York on the night of January 6, 1866, and was got up with a view to exhibit the sympathies of the American people for the South American Republics, and especially Chili.

V. A short description of a political banquet offered, on the 6th of December, to the Press of New York, and to the Spanish-American diplomatists residing in this city, together with some remarks made by Mr. Vicuña Mackenna at the monthly meeting of the *Union League Club of New York*, on the night of the 14th of December, on the Telegraphs of Chile ; and lastly

VI. A short biography of Abraham Lincoln, 16th President of the United States, written in Chili, with the purpose of exhibiting the feelings of the Chilean nation towards the United States in the hour of her most critical trials

In the form of an Appendix, we publish some other documents relating to the main subject of this pamphlet.

THE
REPUBLIC OF CHILI,

ITS PRESENT CONDITION AND PROSPECTS.

(An outline of her Geography, Geology, Social Manners, Political Institutions, Mineral and Agricultural Wealth, Commerce, Statistics, Public Education, Rail-Roads, and Hints on her present War with Spain.)

A LECTURE BEFORE THE TRAVELER'S CLUB OF NEW YORK, ON THE "PRESENT CONDITION AND PROSPECTS OF CHILI," BY B. VICUÑA MACKENNA.

Last Saturday evening, December 2d, 1865, a select and numerous assembly of ladies and gentlemen met at the elegant apartments of the Traveler's Club of New York, on special invitation, to hear a lecture on Chili by Hon. B. Vicuña Mackenna, special envoy of that republic to the United States. The lecturer having been introduced by Mr. Dunbar, President of the Committee of Directors of the Club, proceeded to deliver his lecture in the following terms, in the English language :

LADIES AND GENTLEMEN : I am afraid I have undertaken an enterprise beyond my abilities in addressing you on "The Present State and Prospects of Chili," my beloved country. It is true that I have been accustomed to address large assemblies, but this is the first time I have dared to speak in the presence of ladies, or in a language not familiar to me. But I have surrendered myself to the kind invitation of the Traveler's Club, and undertaken the duty of serving my country in the best way possible for a foreigner in a hospitable land, and to that kindness and indulgence that is always the accompaniment of beauty and talent.

Permit me now, as an introductory remark, to point out
to you some of the more peculiar topographical features
of Chili, and which, I hope, will explain to you many
facts and particular traits of our nation as a people, and as
a prominent member of the family of South American Republics.

In the first place, Chili has its boundaries laid out, as if
by the hand of God, for forming a single nation, a people
of a peculiar and defined character, a family, I dare say,
of good and noble citizens. Chili has no neighbors, properly speaking. Its limits are almost impassable to all
nations. On the east the lofty Andes, covered with eternal snow ; at the north the desert of Atacama, a wilderness of six hundred miles, where neither man nor animal,
nor even the hardiest of plants can live ; on the south the
boundless plains of savage and unknown Patagonia ; on
the west, its only vulnerable side, the mighty Pacific
Ocean.

To this particular and almost isolated geographical position of Chili, and to its mountainous formation, have
been attributed, by both the historian and the philosophi-
cal naturalist, the love of liberty and independence exhibited by her sons—a feeling which appears common to all
peoples who live by themselves and for themselves. To
the same causes may be ascribed that boundless patriotism
of my countrymen, developed in such a unanimous and
earnest manner on the very day when old and fast-decaying
Spain unfolded her flag—so many times beaten by us—in
new defiance of our honor and our power. (Hear, hear.)

UNITY OF RACES.

In the next place, Chili enjoys the great privilege of
unity of race. Far from tropical climates, we did not in-
cur that great calamity of greater nations—slavery ; and,
at the same time, the Spanish conquerors, finding in the
proud and brave Araucanians and Promacas, the natives
of the land, a race worthy of theirs, became intermixed
with them in such a manner that to find in Chili an Indian or a negro is a thing next to impossible. In fact,
small negroes are brought from Lima to be kept in the
largest houses of Santiago as an ornamental piece of furniture. It is owing to this that, although we are only two

millions of men, we represent a population almost as great as that of Mexico, which has six millions of Indians, entirely unfitted for civilization, and, in fact, more inclined to oppose than to accept it.

VARIETY OF CLIMATE.

In the third place, Chili possesses all varieties of climate, from the warm and semi-tropical valleys of Copiapó to the frozen regions of the Archipelago of Chiloe. So it is that at the same time are flowering, under a pure and diaphanous sky, the banana and the pineapple in the north, the peach and the watermellon in the central valleys, and the fruits of the piñones, or fir-pines, in its southern limits. It is to these circumstances, probably, that Chili is indebted for the name of the "Italy of South America," although it has also been called by some kind traveler, who wished to explain the name of our principal port, Valparaiso—"the Valley of Paradise." At least the Chilian ladies believe, as a matter of faith, that they are living in the spot first inhabited by Eve ; and I may add that the immense woods of wild apple trees which cover our southern provinces give some reason for their romantic belief. (Applause.)

IMMENSE EXTENSION OF COAST.

There is another peculiarity of the physical structure of Chili—its immense extent of coast of more than two thousand miles, indented by hundreds of ports and bays, which make the country fitted for carrying on, throughout its entire extent, an active and profitable commerce with the rest of the world. In fact, internal locomotion in Chili is almost unnecessary ; and so near are the Andes to the coast, that a witty Venezuelan critic, the tutor of Bolivar, used to say, "that the country being so narrow, the Chilians were obliged to cling with their nails to the sides of the Andes to avoid falling into the sea." But I make this remark only to show you how easy it is for the foreigner to reach our country without any expenses of inland traveling and settling, and to point out what splendid prospects are there open to foreign emigration.

And that is the very country, ladies and gentlemen, with such boundless extent of shores, that the Spanish Admiral Pareja dares to declare is generally and completely blockaded with five old frigates, when it is in the memory of every one that you needed no less than 462 ships to keep up a blockade (not always effective) of just the same extent of sea-coast during your late gigantic war. Pareja declared the blockade of all our ports, which are sixty or seventy, and do you know how the Government of Chili answered that ridiculous threat? Declaring free and accessible to all nations sixty or seventy ports more.

But in the present age, when Don Quixote is dead and buried for ever in La Mancha, with all the pride and chivalry of the old Castilians, the invention of steam has, it seems, brought them to sea; and there is Admiral Pareja, the Don Quixote of the Pacific, trying to shut up to the commerce of the world no less than a hundred ports with a fleet of five frigates! The story of the wind-mills recurs to every one. (Laughter.) But I have now, with your kind permission, to follow steadily the thread of my lecture.

PARTICULAR INFLUENCE OF THE OCEAN.

There is yet something worthy of your notice in the formation of Chili. Exposed as it is in its whole extent and widely open to the direct influence of the Pacific Ocean, the soil derives from its grateful breezes a robust and wholesome vegetation, which covers her fields with carpets of flowers and boundless prairies of pasturage. This climatogical peculiarity is most striking when the traveler to Chili from the east of the Andes crosses from that petrified ocean of earth called the "Pampas of Buenos Ayres." There, on the oriental side of the lofty mountains, every trace of natural vegetation disappears, as if Chili was ambitiously taking for itself, and pumping into the other side, that moisture from the surface of the ocean which renders rich and beautiful her plains and valleys. It is supposed at the same time, that the elasticity of the atmosphere along the shores of Chili has a certain influence on the minds of the people—giving a more acute intelligence to those living in the vicinity of the ocean than the inhabitants of the interior enjoy. That was, at least, the opinion of an old Jesuit historian, MIGUEL DE OLIVAREZ, who probably lived on the sea coast.

GEOLOGY OF CHILI.

I will devote a moment to giving you a passing idea of the general geological formation of Chili. No country has, perhaps, more to interest the modern geologist than that unexplored region. With the exception of the German traveler MEYER, the eminent English naturalist DARWIN, and our Professor PISSIS, nobody has devoted even a superficial study to that branch of science in our country. If the famous LYELL, or Prof. AGASSIZ, now busily engaged on the banks of the Amazones, had visited our shores, many important discoveries would have been added to that beautiful science.

But, nevertheless, it is clearly demonstrated from what is now known that Chili is quite a modern country. There are, indeed, persons still living who, I can properly say, have seen it growing, and coming but as a new-born giant from the bottom of the sea. The phenomenon of the gradual rising of the shores, which has been observed as well in Norway and in some other parts of the world, is plainly visible in Chili. Admiral FITZROY saw it with his own eyes, when the earthquake of 1835 (the last severe one we have experienced) took place. In a few minutes the land was raised in some places many feet; a small island appeared in the bay of Talcahuano, and so uniform was and is yet continuing to be this gradual rising of the land, that the theatre of Valparaiso stands now in a place that thirty years ago formed part of the anchorage for ships.

These facts prove, in my humble opinion, that Chili is quite a new country, comparatively, and as far as I know, no traces have ever been found within its limits of an age previous to the tertiary period. The general opinion that the Andes belong to the last epochs of the formation of the earth, is entirely confirmed in the Chilian system of those prodigious mountains.

And upon that matter allow me to relate a very simple fact which illustrates fully in its own simplicity the tremendous revolution which that part of the Continent has gone through. The geologist Darwin found, in 1837, in the pass of the Pinquenes, at the elevation of 15,000 feet, the trunk of a pine standing with its roots firm on the rocks, and saturated with marine salts and incrustations of shells. The trunk was cut, brought to England, and there the analysis proved that it had been under the water of the sea for many years, perhaps centuries.

Well, now, the conclusions that we derive from that modest discovery are very striking. In the first place, it shows that the tree had existed in firm land where it first put out its roots. Next, by some powerful change of the earth, shaken by volcanic action, the land was submerged, when the tree got petrified with marine salts, and afterward was again uplifted to the immense height in which it was found. It is, perhaps, interesting to know that that kind of tree does not now exist in the same latitude.

THE THREE KINGDOMS OF NATURE.

I wished, gentlemen, to be able to entertain you at length about the beauties and marvels of Chili, and its resources in the three kingdoms of nature, from the humble *calceolaria*, a wild flower of Chili, admired by all the lovers of gardening, to the gigantic palm tree (*jubea spectabilis*), indigenous to Chili, worthy of taking a place among the tallest trees of the California or Nevada forests.

But that course would take us a long distance from our principal purpose, and I beg your kind permission to pass over any picturesque description, and limit myself to point out the general outlines of the land, although I am afraid of fatiguing you with the dryness of my discourse. [No, no. Go on !]

I will only call your attention to a more decided physical feature of Chili, in order to explain to you more clearly the general aspect of the country.

A perfect line of separation divides, and, indeed, nearly in the centre, two very different portions of the land. That line is the beautiful valley of the Aconcagua, which was properly called "Chili" in the time of the Spanish conquest.

To the north of that valley the country is formed by a series of high granite and basaltic chains that descend transversely from the Andes to the sea, and are cut at proportional distances by deep and narrow valleys, teeming with vegetation and villages thickly populated. These are the valleys of Copiapó, so famous by its immense production of silver ; next, the valley of Coquimbo, which produces perhaps half of the copper that comes every year into the markets of the world, and the valleys of Huasco, Ligua and Petorca, noted for the abundance of gold they produced in the time of the Spaniards.

I cannot give you the exact statistics of the immense wealth buried in those northern mountains, but some facts that I will take the liberty of mentioning to you hereafter will give you some idea of the marvelous profits which those localities offer to industry and capital. Southward of the Aconcagua valley the structure of the territory changes entirely. The mountains disappear and a series of magnificent broad valleys, which were undoubtedly large geographical basins and lakes, now converted into real gardens of cultivation, come to sight.

The first of these large valleys, which preserves the form of an immense lake drained by nature, is that of the Mapocho, in the centre of which lies the beautiful capital of Chili, and is, perhaps, 200 miles in circumference. Next follows that of Rancagua; next that of Colchagua, and so forth up to the mighty Biobió, now navigated by steamers, which is the boundary of civilized Chili. To those who have visited the plains of Lombardy or glanced over the valley of Mexico from the heights of the Sierra Madre, the view of the Chilian valleys will undoubtedly bring to their minds pleasant recollections and comparisons, the endless rows of poplar trees and a real net of irrigating canals being the principal features of the landscape.

And here another trait of the physiognomy of the country comes out. The immense plains of the Araucania, whose wild and brave children live and die on the back of their swift horses, worthy yet by their courage and their indisputable love of their native land, of the finest and most beautiful of Spanish poems—the Araucana.

Further to the southern extremity of those plains begins what we might call the fourth system of the topography of Chili, the primitive mountains which the human foot has never trod, and the immense rivers and lakes not yet explored by science.

The last aspect of the country is afforded by the barren and endless plains of Patagonia, which extend from the limits of the province of Llanquihue to the settlement of Punta Arenas, in the Straits of Magellan, a place well known to all the American navigators who choose to go through that passage between the two oceans.

WEALTH IN SILVER.

Now permit me to make a very rapid inland tour from Copiapó down to Valdivia, in order to point out to you some of the more prominent features of the principal provinces into which Chili is divided, being fourteen in number.

On a chily night, thirty years ago, a shepherd made a
fire in the mountains of Copiapó, and next morning he
saw at his feet a stream of silver, which the heat had
melted. That was the discovery of the mines of Copiapó,
which have produced in thirty years more than $100,000,-
000. Now they are rather in the decay; but the produce
of the last year was $1,638,272—a sum inferior to that
of Guanajuato and Real del Monte, which the anonymous
and ominous company of Napoleon and Maximilian wishes
to develop, against the decided opinion of the old and glorious President Monroe.

IMMENSE PRODUCTION OF COPPER.

Next follows the province of Coquimbo, whose capital,
the beautiful town of La Serena rests, a real syren at the
foot of the hills by the sea side, supporting a population
of thirty thousand inhabitants, and containing some of
the most beautiful and syren-like daughters of Chili.

The wealth of that province is almost indescribable.
There is, indeed, a mountain, that of Famaya, formed, if
it could be so said, of pure copper ore. The value of this
single product, as it is manufactured in Chili, was, in
1864, $9,506,957, and that of the copper regulus, or
in its more imperfect state, $4,716,912, making in the
whole (and not taking in consideration the raw ore sent
to England, and which is worth several millions), the immense amount of $14,221,849.

Now you will be able to form an idea of the deep alarm
awakened in England on the arrival of the the news that
through the mere wicked and cowardly caprice of a vulgar sailor, such a fountain of so valuable and indispensa-
ble an article was shut off from the commerce and urgent
necessities of the world. The London *Times*, denouncing
to all civilized nations, in warm and eloquent language,
the unwarrantable conduct of Spain, declares in its leading article of the 19th inst., that out of 498,780 cwt. of
manufactured copper imported last year into England,
304,380 cwt., that is to say, more than two-thirds, came
from Chili, and that out of 25,000 tons of regulus 22,000
tons, or almost the whole quantity, came from that source.

And now I beg to ask, in the presence of these data, if
such a country, young, energetic, and industrious,
and which sends to Europe every year more than twenty
millions of dollars, in only two standard articles, is to be

conquered, to be humiliated by Spain, ruled, as she is, by a corrupt court, without credit whatever in the markets of the world, and whose name is perpetually placed on the black slate of the hopeless debtors, at the very hour that the bonds of Chili are quoted at a higher rate than those of any other nation, England, France, or the United States included? (Long applause.)

ITS AGRICULTURAL WEALTH.

Now, I will detain you a little while in Santiago, the capital of Chili, as the remainder of the country southward is merely a rich but mountainous series of agricultural valleys and plains, with large but rather dull old-fashioned Spanish towns. It will be interesting, nevertheless, to establish the fact that this part of the country after providing liberally for the interior wants of all classes, leaves a surplus of flour and wheat of the value of millions of dollars, which are paid to us by Peru, Brazil, and even England. The statistical report of last year shows an exportation of $2,231,090 flour, and $1,039,071 wheat. In the golden days of the discovery of California these values amounted to several millions more, being ourselves during three or four years, the sole source of agricultural supplies for El Dorado.

THE SOCIETY OF CHILI.

Let us now rest for a while in the capital of Chili, the sunny land of my boyhood, where my heart first beat to the tender feelings of hope and love, and where yet God is willing to rejoice my home with the presence of all that there is dear in life, fathers, brothers, friends. [Applause.]

But before going any further in the social consideration of my native land, I will call your kind attention to a very singular idea prevailing in this country, and almost everywhere in the Atlantic nations, and about the habits, morals, and social condition of the South American republics. The other day a friend of mine, and a man of undoubted superiority in this country, looking at my clothes in Broadway, asked me with surprise, if such things were used in Chili, or if I had bought them in New York. [Great laughter.]

But the explanation of these curious errors consists in the fact that a great majority of the people forming their ideas through reading novels and sensation books, believe

us to be pure Indians, as those described by the masterly
pen of Cooper ; or cavaliers of the style of the old conquerors of Peru and Mexico, so admirably described by
Irving and Prescott, and who adored only two things
during their dark days, the Inquisition and the bull-fight.
[Laughter.]

But the truth is, that we live, dress, eat, walk, drive,
and expend our money in much the same way that
the sons of the beautiful and mighty Manhattan Island
dress, drive, and spend their money. (Laughter.) The
only substantial difference being, I must say, that there
the mildness of the climate permits us to use more light
clothing, for although Crinoline has already imposed her
despotic rule, the ladies of Santiago do not yet wear *hooks*
and *waterfalls.* (Laughter and applause.) it may be
possible, though, that Pareja will let them have some nice
hooks out of his old flagship, the *Villa de Madrid.* . .

SANTIAGO.

Santiago possesses a theatre which is considered the third
in the world after that of San Carlos of Naples, and the
Scala of Milan, by its immense proportions, having been
built ten years ago at an expense of nearly $400,000; and
I mention these circumstances only to give a small proof
of the taste and comforts of life in that capital of 120,000
inhabitants, which contains 5,000 large houses, possesses
more bronze statues of national heroes than the imperial
city of New York, and supports in luxurious garb few less
churches than Rome itself. But, gentlemen, upon this
matter it will appear to me something like a shame to try
to convince you that we are a civilized community, and at
the same time to contradict the foolish and childish stories
of vulgar travelers. About this class of informants, I
will say only that I know a single one sincere and earnest
in what he tells about my country. I refer to the well-
known German traveler, Gerstaker, once a fireman on a
Mississippi steamer, and who, having seen some of the
large courts of our houses in Santiago paved with small
bones, forming beautiful ornamental patterns, declares
solemnly that the vindictive character of the Chilians has
led them to pave their houses with the bones of the Spaniards killed in the war of Independence. (Laughter.)

Now, passing from society to the political institutions of the country, I will only mention that Chili was discovered in 1535 by Diego de Almagro, about fifty years after the first voyage of Columbus. That great soldier, Pedro Valdivia, conquered the Indians north of the Biobio, in a war of more than ten years' duration, in which he himself fell a victim, and that since those days up to the beginning of the present century, Chili, like all the Spanish colonies, has slept a melancholy and undisturbed sleep, but yet a long, long, miserable dream of slavery, darkness, and humiliation.

During two centuries, indeed, there did not exist more life in those countries than that lent by Spain itself, once a year, when the *galeon* arrived with all the goods and all the news for the coming twelve months. The only historical record of those days is of a dispute between the judges and the canons for the precedence of seats in public festivals or processions, the burning of a wealthy heretic, or the prayer-days fixed upon by proper authority, when the news was brought that some of the chaste Bourbon princesses or queens were to be delivered of a prince or princess. (Laughter.)

And it is to those days that Spain desires now to bring again her lost sons on this side of the water. And she has attacked successively San Domingo, Mexico, Peru, and Chili, forgetting that she has already a grown-up daughter much nearer to us than to her, and to which, perhaps, in no distant day, we shall pay our compliments, being ourselves ready to receive her at any time in the common home of the American Republics, and she quite ready to come. (Long and enthusiastic applause.)

But that state of things did not last long with us. The influence of the French revolution of '89, the old wrongs of Spain to our country, the secret support of commercial and enterprising England, and above all things, the direct pressure of the independence of the North American colonies, brought us to a war with Spain.

That war lasted sixteen years. Spain was beaten every day on all the shores, in all the mountains, in all the valleys of South America, and at last Bolivar and San Martin, our two great liberators, standing like the giants of the Andes in the plains of Ayacucho, on the 9th of December

1824, out for ever, with the sword of victory, the hateful bond of colonial royalty.

INFLUENCE OF THE UNITED STATES.

I have just mentioned that the independence of the United States forcibly aided ours, and I hope I shall be allowed to state that since those days the influence of American institutions (if not of all American Presidents and Cabinets) has been powerfully reflected in our public life. Madison and his great secretary, James Monroe, were the first to come to our help. The earliest diplomatic agent ever sent to the revolutionary colonies was the famous Joel Poinsett, of North Carolina, who fought with us our own battles.

Next to that, the American Government, passing from the sympathy of principles to the responsibility of doctrine, wrote in the infallible code of her public institutions, and of her own existence as a nation, those two principles, which shall live as long as there will be life and honor in the country of George Washington and of Abraham Lincoln, viz :

1st—" The American continents, by the free and independent conditions which they have assumed and maintained, are henceforth not to be considered as subjects for future colonization by any European Power.

2nd—" The United States consider any attempt on the part of European Powers to extend their system to any portion of this hemisphere *as dangerous to their peace and safety.*"

HONORS PAID TO WASHINGTON AND LINCOLN.

And in this part of my discourse, I beg leave to halt for a while, and take the liberty of reading to you a brief paragraph from a speech delivered in behalf of the interests of the United States, on the eve of the Fourth of July, of 1864, in the Chilian Congress, of which I had the honor of being a member, and which translated faithfully will wholly explain my thoughts.

" But allow me, at least," I said on that occasion to my fellow-Representatives, " to bring to your mind that since the United States became a free nation, that is to say, since they ceased to be a mere appendix to a monarchy, they have always stretched out to us the hand of friendship and of brotherhood. They sent to us, in 1812, the first printing establishment, by which means the early light of our freedom broke out among us. They were the first to accredit a diplomatic agent to our country, Consul Poinsett, who enlisted as a volunteer in our revolutionary army. They furnished General Carrera with a fleet worth over a million of dollars, though he landed on this soil a poor, proscribed, and unknown man. All their great statesmen have been ardent friends of South America.—Madison acknowledged our independence ; Adams cooperated with Bolivar to lay down the basis of American Union at the Congress of Panama ; Monroe raised up the protecting shield of his famous doctrine over both continents; and lately, the honest and immortal Abraham Lincoln, the rail-splitter, dispatched friendly messengers to each of the Spanish-American Republics to settle their old difficulties with the United States."

And further, let me add, that when the appalling martyrdom of this great magistrate reached my country, I saw many, many tears in my own home, and many, many pale and mournful faces everywhere, as a testimony of how pure and how sincere was our love for that new redeemer of mankind. For myself, I take the liberty of stating that I wrote a short biography of that eminent man, and moved in the House of Representatives a law, to be passed according to the following resolutions, which I copy from the Journal of Congress :

"*Resolved*, That the portraits of George Washington and of Abraham Lincoln, the first and last Presidents of the United States of America, be executed at the expense of the nation, and placed on the walls of the reception-room of the Minister of Foreign Affairs, as a tribute rendered by the Chilian people to those of the United States, on the occasion of the happy re-establishment of their internal peace, and as a remembrance of the sorrowful loss suffered in the death of their first magistrate.

"*Resolved*, That this resolution be inscribed, as an appropriate motto, at the foot of the aforesaid portraits, and that it be communicated by the Government of Chili to the President of the Senate and House of Representatives of the United States, as an expression of the sentiments of the Chilian Congress."

(Loud and prolonged cheers.)

Such were the feelings, the ideas, the sympathies of the two countries, so taking every one by surprise, and

2

the whole country unarmed. What will these feelings be in the future.? Gentlemen, that is a question
which it does not belong to me to answer. There is a
mighty people in this country, there is a Congress replen-
ished from the whole intelligence and good and honest
hearts of the land, there is a noble-minded President full
of confidence in the will of his fellow-citizens, and it is
for them to answer and to solve such a question.

But I observe that I have digressed a little from my
original plan of showing you the present condition of
Chili and its prospects for the future, and now I return
again fully to my path.

GOVERNMENT AND POLITICAL INSTITUTIONS.

Chili having won her independence, with the best blood
of her sons, devoted herself to the fruitful labors of
peace and industry ; gave herself a constitution based on
the general principles of self-government, with a President
eligible every five years, with a House of Representatives
returnable every three years, and a Senate of twenty
members to be elected every seven years. Every community of twenty thousand inhabitants is entitled to
return a member of the House, and the Senators are elected by provinces. The President governs, with a responsible Cabinet of four Secretaries and a Council of State,
appointed from among the most distinguished persons in
the community.

Chili is perhaps the country in the whole world least
taxed, 90 cents being the average proportion of taxes
among all classes of individuals ; and yet those taxes are
voted only every eighteen months by Congress.

The duties on foreign goods are high only in the articles of luxury, and free or slightly taxed when of general use. In a comparative statement of the duties paid in
the Custom-houses of France, England, the United States,
and Chili, made lately by the eminent French economist,
Courselles de Seneuil, it is ascertained that the latter country is by far the more liberal. It is owing, probably, to
this liberality that the Custom-house in Valparaiso produced in 1863 $4,259,533.

The administration of justice is organized very much on
the same footing as that of the United States, with a
Supreme Court at its head. There is, nevertheless, one

substantial difference—the Supreme Court of Chili has no political power whatever, and all the members of the judicial body are nominated by the President for life. In a particular branch of the administration of justice, Chili possesses, it seems to me, a great advantage.— We have a general code of law framed on the plan of the Code Napoleon, and especial codes of commerce, mines, legal proceedings, and criminal law. All have been prepared in the last ten years by eminent lawyers of the country, and are of great service to the republic, as the law is put within the reach of the humblest citizen.

In its political administration, Chili has followed the principles of France, the country undoubtedly best governed as far as the official machinery of power works on the community. There is in existence a Board of Statistics, which issues a report on the progress of the country every year and makes up the general census of the republic every ten years. The last census was carried out all over the country on the 19th of last April, and it is believed, from the reports published, that the actual number of inhabitants will be approximatively two millions, the population doubling every forty years.

LAWS ON FOREIGNERS—EMIGRATION.

The laws of Chili are of the most liberal spirit towards foreigners, as many of the respectable gentlemen in this hall can testify by their own personal experience. They are permitted to do whatever the natives of the country have a right to do, and further, they are not burdened with any personal taxations or duties, even the most trivial. And to this circumstance, and to the similitude of climate, products, and cultivation with the nations of Europe, it is due that Chili offers such splendid prospects to emigrants of all races, except the degraded Asiatics, which have not been permitted to be introduced in the country by the new slaveholders of the Pacific, the importers of miserable colonies of Chinese, or the coolies of the Southern Ocean.

At the outbreak of the war with Spain, the Government was preparing the establishment of a Board of Emigration, on similar principles with those existing in this country, and had already devoted more than half a million of acres in the fertile province of Llanquihue for the settlement of foreign emigrants. There are living now in those regions, in happy condition, more than two thousand Germans. According to the census of 1855, there were in Chili 6,600 Germans, 1,247 English, 1,196 French, only 769 Spaniards, and 571 citizens of the United States, about 20,100 foreigners in all. But in ten years this number has doubtless been doubled.

There is another consideration of importance connected with our population. There do not exist in Chili idle classes. All people are obliged to work to get their living, and they work hard indeed in the deep bottoms of the copper-mines of Atacama, in the northern extremity of the land, and in the inexhaustible coal-fields of Lota and Coronel, which by their extent and accessibility are not surpassed by any in England or France.

THE ARMY.

At the same time, the regular army of Chili is comparatively small, and is kept occupied (as was yours before the war) in protecting the frontiers against the invasion of the wild Araucanian Indians. But we possess, in fact, a national army of more than 80,000 men, both horse and foot, registered on our military roll, and which could take the field, as they have already done in some measure, at the first warning of the country's danger.

CHARITIES.

The benevolent institutions of the country are worthy of a particular study, as they exhibit the general disposition of the Chilians to practice the virtues of hospitality. To avoid, however, minute explanation on this subject, I should recommend you to read a chapter consecrated to this matter by Dr. Baxlay, a well-meaning traveler, who visited Chili two or three years ago, and has just published an interesting book on South America.

PRINCIPLES OF SELF-GOVERNMENT.

The public institutions that belong properly to the organization of self-government, work in Chili with as perfect ease as is exhibited so gloriously in this country. The rights of associations, the liberty of the press, the irresponsibility of the opinions of the representatives of the country in Congress, the liberty of conscience, that last conquest of progress and justice, the trial by jury, the privilege of *habeas corpus*, and, in fact, all the modern liberties and franchises of democracy, are in full and active operation in our country.

JOURNALS.

I might as well add, apropos of the press, that although we have no papers so interesting as those of New-York, we nevertheless publish some of the largest and best edited journals of South America, and some as old as are printed on the Southern continent. The Valparaiso *Mercury*, and some interesting and active political papers as the *Ferrocarril* of Santiago, a magnificent journal kept up in the French style of publication.

This is, gentlemen, the general condition of the country at large, but there are yet three questions to which I request your patient attention for a few minutes, as they are the foundation of the actual civilization of nations ; *first*, the public education of the people ; *second*, the extent of the railroads, and *third*, the extent of its commerce and interchanges with the other countries of the world.

PUBLIC EDUCATION.

Chili has pursued a most steady course in educating its own people, knowing that therein consists the true support of democracy and self-government. Her Institute or University of Santiago, is considered the most important of South America, and more than a dozen learned European professors have been engaged for the purpose of spreading the knowledge of the highest branches of science. At an expense of more than $100,000 the Chilian Government maintains an Astronomical Observatory, the only one existing in the Southern hemisphere, and has consequently done great service to modern astronomy. There existed in 1862, the last epoch of the official statistics now in my power, 5,792 students of professional careers, most of them in the National Institute of Santiago, and in the provincial lyceums—every province having an institution of this kind for herself. In 1810, in the good old times of mother Spain, there existed only two public schools in the kingdom, and in 1862 this number had increased to 933. Of these 588 belonged to the male sex, and 345 to the female, being 23,563 of the first, and 12,412 of the last—35,975 in all of persons educated at the expense of the State. Chili devotes ONE-TENTH of its revenue to public instruction—[long applause]—and there existed a President who was elected in 1851, having adopted as the platform of his canvassing this single principle, "*Popular education.*" [Loud cheers]

RAILWAYS.

In the progress of steam locomotion Chili stands so high that you will be surprised on hearing that only four countries—the United States, England, France, and Germany—possess greater extent of railroad, taking into consideration the size of the respective countries, Chili possesses at present six main lines of railways.

The northern one connects the port of Caldera with the silver regions of Copiapó, and was the first ever built in South America (1850,) previous to the erection of the line of Panamá, which has, like the last, an extent of forty-seven miles. The second is that of Carrizal, twenty-four miles in length. It has been built by Americans and native capitalists for bringing to the sea-shore the rich copper ores of the interior.

The third is much more important, as it runs south from La Serena, the capital of Coquimbo, and is intended to connect with that between Valparaiso and Santiago, a distance of about five hundred miles south. Of this line ninety miles are complete, and as many in course of progress.

The fourth is the famous railway between Valparaiso and Santiago, over immense mountains, built at an expense of twelve millions of dollars. It was laid out by the eminent American civil engineer, Allen Campbell, now residing in this city in a very high position, and completed, as a contractor, by another American of great enterprise, and generous heart, Henry Meiggs. This line extends for more than 135 miles over a rough country, and is considered a work inferior to none for its boldness and solidity.

The fifth line extends from Santiago, through the inland valleys and over level ground, to San Fernando, a distance equal to that between Valparaiso and Santiago, but, passing through a highly cultivated plain, it has cost only half the amount of the last. A distinguished American engineer, Col. Walter W. Evans, now of this city, was the builder of this railway. And as in passing I mentioned the names of some Americans prominent among us, let me pay a tribute of respect and affection to a noble and intelligent man, a real embodiment of the most characteristic qualities of the American people—to Hon. Thomas Horace Nelson—the last Minister of the United States in Chili, and who has gained the sincere affection of my countrymen, both by his personal and official attainments.

Lately, grants for four new branches of railroads were made by the Legislature, and the line going southward from Santiago will be extended this summer to Curicó, at an expense of nearly $1,500,000.

The purpose of the government is to build a central line between Santiago and Concepcion, on the banks of the Biobio, a distance of about 600 miles, of which, there are 150 completed, the whole of the country having been carefully surveyed. The actual value of the railways of the country, which measure nearly 500 miles, is $30,000,000, and it is thought that an the expense of less than that amount, a complete line of rails will be run from La Serena to Concepcion, (a distance of more than 1,000 miles,) and all within the course of ten or fifteen years.

When this great work, to which the country and Congress have lent their utmost support is completed, Chili cannot but be the best organized and best protected against internal or foreign foes of all other countries. Lines of telegraph run parallel to all the railways, and the very day war was declared against Spain orders were given to extend the magnetic wire from the northern to the southern extremity of the country, which work has been undertaken with unabated energy. And that, gentlemen, has been the answer of the country to the piratical assault of the Spanish Admiral. He wished to put a gag in our mouths by shutting the doors of the country, and the country has used the inextinguishable voice of steam and electricity to carry all over the land her will, her dignity, and the resolution of opposing Spain to the last breath of life. (Applause.)

COMMERCE.

I wish to impress upon the minds of the thinking men, who have honored me by listening to this long and wearisome lecture, the importance of the commerce of Chili, in order to show how little has been done by the American people, and, I must say, by the American Government, to develop the interests of this nation in those far but rich countries. The value of goods imported into Chili in 1864, according to official statistics, was $18,867,363 ; and would any of you believe that in this commerce, of which you might have as good a share as any other nation, England is represented by forty-three per cent., while the enterprising, the prosperous and active people of the United States, with their enormous, crowded, and countless manufactures, stand only in the proportion of *five per cent* ? But that is a fact, according to late official returns, and I may add, as far as my personal knowledge goes, that there exist in Valparaiso, among hundreds of large European houses of commerce, only three American firms—that of the old and respectable house of Alsop & Co., and those of A. Hemenway & Co. and Loring & Co.

The exports of Chili last year were to the value of $27,242,853, leaving in our favor a balance in trade of more than $8,000,000.

The internal commerce of the country, which is free to all flags (hear, hear,) amounted to $28,896,783, being an increase of $12,199,862 over that of 1861, and reaching in its whole extent, and without taking into consideration the commerce in transit to the Argentine Republic, Bolivia, and Perú, which amount to many millions, the sum of $75,005,000.

FINANCES.

The public revenue of the present year was calculated before the war at $10,000,000, and as the foreign debt of the Government, always faithfully paid, is less than $8,000,000, it can be said that no country is in better condition as to finance. Now, if we take into consideration that the nation owns more than half the railways, and is free to sell that part to individuals, it could further be said that Chili has no foreign debt whatever. I think it necessary to add that paper was there unknown as official currency. But lately war has obliged the banks to make a paper issue of $4,000,000, guaranteed, nevertheless, by more than twenty millions of coin and other securities.— We have been obliged, at the same time, to raise in England a loan of six millions of dollars for war purposes, and an equal amount of money was to be collected in the country.

Such, ladies and gentlemen, were the conditions and prospects of Chili when a man, whose name the world had never heard before, came one morning, surprising our good faith, and taking cowardly and villainous advantage of the defenceless condition of our shores, to stop that marvelous march of progress, and overthrow in a minute the work of so many years of patient industry and honesty.

THE WAR WITH SPAIN.

One word more upon the question of this war, and I have done.

Who understands the causes of this war between Chili and Spain? I think nobody, not even myself, as there never was in the history of nations a war so groundless and ridiculous as this is on the part of Spain.

But as the causes of this difficulty have never been properly understood, and as the day before yesterday one of the leading and most influential papers of this city expressed a wish that no sympathy should be bestowed upon us, on the ground that the facts were not yet fully known, I will endeavor to put them before you in their full light, begging of you one moment more of patience.

On the 24th of April, 1863, a day of sad record for America, both North and South, Admiral Pinzon, on the part of Spain, seized the Chincha Islands, belonging to Peru, and declared in a public manifesto that in doing so he *revindicated the property of Spain, as there was only a state of truce with Peru since the truce of Ayacucho in 1824.*

At such an extraordinary avowal, the whole of South America rose in alarm, and stood like a single man by the side of their attacked brother. They acted, it is true, in their own behalf at the same time, as they might also be "revindicated at any moment, especially Chili, the nearest neighbor of the invaded country, and the people who had twice stood by Peru in her fight for liberty, the cause of the two countries being one.

A warm feeling of sympathy was consequently awakened in Chili in favor of Perú. The press violently attacked Spain; volunteers went over to Perú; and coal was declared contraband of war for both parties, as it was impossible to provide with means of attack the very enemy that was preying like a highway robber on our coast. And I ask you, gentlemen, what country on the surface of the earth would have acted otherwise? Would you? Would you restrain your press on the affairs of Mexico, and deny your sympathies for the institutions and the men of a country which in some respects forms a part of your own? Besides, as I had occasion to develop fully, at an address I delivered a few days ago at Panamá, and which many of you probably read in the New York *Herald* of last week, there was no ground whatever, in the presence of the most stringent principles of international law, not only for a war, but even for a diplomatic rupture.

PERÚ TO STAND BY CHILI IN WAR ALLIANCE.

But as only a pretext was needed, as soon as the difficulty between Spain and Perú was settled in such a disgraceful manner, that the whole country rose against the traitors with the blush in their face, Pareja undertook to ask explanations of our Government for the legitimate acts and for the innocent sympathies shown to our suffering brothers. And let me pause a moment in my narrative, to inform you, in the joy of my heart, that the noble revolution of Perú triumphed by its national force with little bloodshed, at the gates of Lima, on the 5th of November last, as we have just heard by the steamer arrived this evening from Aspinwall.

Thanks to God, there are no more traitors in America; and I take upon myself to declare, as a friend of Generals Canseco and Prado, the President and the leader of that glorious protest against Spain, that Perú will now stretch out to Chili the hand of a brother, and repay the sacrifices to her cause. Yes, gentlemen, I feel authorized to declare in this responsible place, that the new Government of Perú *is bound by the most solemn pledges of nations to declare war, immediate and active war, against Spain.*

Such is the fact at this very hour, and you may rely upon it, as I come to this country from the head-quarters of the Peruvian army and revolutionary fleet. I beg to add that the *Express* of to-day makes a very singular mistake in declaring that the new Government of Perú comes back on a *Spanish platform*, when the very reverse is the fact, as the revolution sprang out of the infamous conduct of the last government of Ex-Gen. Pezet, a traitor, like Santana and Almonte, to the noble cause of America.

The asking of explanations from our government by Pareja, was in itself an act of insult on the part of the agent of Spain, as we were the party offended. But the Chilian Government, giving a proof of its prudence and forbearance, gave the explanations required, to such an extent that the claimant declared himself in a public dispatch, and in benalf of his government, entirely satisfied.

That event took place in May last, and both the country and the government had entirely forgotten the past question, when suddenly, on the morning of the 12th of September, a small steamer chartered by our Minister in Lima, cast her anchor in Valparaiso, bearing extraordinary news. The Government of Spain had declared *insufficient* the satisfaction accepted as fully satisfactory by her public representative had recalled him in disgrace, and ordered Pareja (the secret abettor of the plot,) to go with the whole of his fleet to impose upon us the shame of humiliating our honor and our flag to the guns of his ships. This course was made yet more insolent, as we know that Pareja and half a dozen intriguing and lawless men surrounding him, had been the active agents for obtaining from the Spanish Government the authorization of their villainous attack upon Chili. Pareja was so proud with his old frigates, and particularly as we had none at that time, that he wrote to his beloved Queen that in less than a quarter of an hour he would settle the difficulty with little Chili.

But the poor old Admiral was miserably mistaken. At the very moment of his appearance in the bay of Valparaiso, the country—as a single thought, as a single soul, as a single arm—roused itself to the support of the government, and offered life and property to maintain its honor, so infamously and cowardly assailed. Consequently, the very day that Pareja declared the blockade, and took violent possession of a few of our merchant ships, who had not yet changed their flags, both Houses of Congress met spontaneously on the 24th of September. War was declared immediately against Spain by the unanimous vote of all present ; the government was authorized to raise a loan of $20,000,000 ; to call to arms whatever troops deemed necessary ; to increase, or, more properly speaking, create a navy by all means available, and carry immediate and active hostilities against the insolent invaders.

And now, gentlemen, I ask you candidly and honestly, would you, could you, as members of an independent and free country, have done otherwise ? [Cries of no, no.]

CHILI NOTHING TO LOOSE BY A WAR WITH SPAIN.

So the war with Spain is one of honor for us, as it is a ridiculous and purposeless ostentation of power and pride on the part of Spain. The English people, excited undoubtedly by their great interest in the Pacific, have understood nevertheless the real position, the origin, and the consequences of this singular and almost enigmatical case, and have severely condemned Spain. It is for you now to give utterance to your opinion, and support it in the interest of your ideas and of the old principles of your glorious republic.

But allow me to say, before I close these last observations, that although we regret, as a civilized country, this war having originated in such extravagant pretexts, we are not in the least afraid of it. Far from that. We have a history and glorious forefathers who taught us how to fight and how to conquer. [Applause.] We have a respectable and respected position among the nations of the world, and that respect is not commanded by armies or fleets, but by our institutions, our credit as a commercial country, and our wealth, superior to many of the old monarchies of Europe, and certainly to that of marauding and bankrupt Spain. And then, gentlemen, war with all its horrors and its calamities, possesses great advantages for new countries. We have nothing to loose by the hate of Spain, and something to gain by it. We are not indebted to Spain in Chili for a single man of enterprise, for a single cent of capital, for any importation of industry. England appears in our commercial section, as I have already stated, as importer in the proportion of 43 per cent. France 20 per cent., Germany 9 per cent., the United States 5 per cent., Peru and Brazil 3 per cent. ; but Spain *for nothing at all!* (Laughter.) There are, too, in Chili, at present, seven hundred Spaniards in all, but all belonging to the classes of little traders ; none to the liberal or even most humble professions.

And I may be allowed to repeat, without paying attention to local considerations, new-born countries require to be at once known in the great fair of the world. You were once only a small nation, and had not a defender among the great peoples of the globe, until you, young and inexperienced, but full of daring with the righteousness of your cause, went to war with England in 1812. You came great and powerful out of that struggle, and so we expect to come out of ours, against our fast-decaying mother country. And mind it, gentlemen, we are ready to go to that war at our own risk, with our own blood, with our own money, without asking any other nation's material help or entangling alliances. What we want is merely justice, the full appreciation of our dignity and of our rights, so that it may not be said that we entered into this war through contemptible notions of pride and vanity, but for the sake of our present existence, our future destinies as a nation, commanding the respect and the sympathies of the civilized world.

And now, ladies and gentlemen, there remains for me only the pleasant duty of offering you my most sincere and earnest thanks for the kindness shown to me on this occasion, and I do so with a grateful heart. (Long applause.)

After the lecture, Mr. E. George Squier moved a vote of thanks to the lecturer, in a few complimentary remarks, which motion was seconded by Mr. James S. Mackie in a brief but happy speech, and carried with signal enthusiasm.

————————•◦•————————

Among several judgments registered by the daily papers of New York upon the present lecture, we consider it becoming to our purpose to reprint the following leading article of the *Evening Post* of December the 12th, and which relates to the commerce between Chili and the United States :

Señor McKenna, special agent of the Chilian government in this country, gave a few days ago an excellent account of his country, in which he related much that was new to his hearers and to the general public, and which is at the same time of great interest and importance to Americans.

After pointing out the fact that Chili has distinct natural boundaries in the Andes, the Pacific Ocean, the great desert of Atacama, and the savage plains of Patagonia ; and that it possesses a homogeneous population, a various but temperate climate, an immense coast line containing hundreds of ports and bays, which make access to the interior easy, a fertile agricultural region, which enables the nation to export breadstuffs, and mineral resources so rich that, besides coal, silver and gold, half the copper produced in the whole world, annually, is mined in Chili. Mr. McKenna described the social and political condition of his country. Chili has two millions of people, who form a republic, in which a president is elected every five years, while the popular branch of the Congress is chosen every three years, and the Senate for seven years. Taxation is trifling, the custom duties are light, and imposed only on articles of luxury; one-tenth of the whole revenue of the state is devoted to public instruction; and in 1862 there were nine hundred and thirty-three free schools in the country, besides a university at Santiago, the most important in South America, and colleges in the different provinces.

Finally, lands are cheap, the climate is fine, the natural products various, the feeling towards foreigners very liberal, the undeveloped wealth immense, the railroads of the country so extended that Chili is excelled in this regard only by the United States, England, France and Germany, and the people are very favorably predisposed towards the United States.

Yet with this country, whose people are so friendly to us, whose institutions are so similar to ours, who seem to be progressing in the same direction with ourselves, and who feel themselves to have the same interests with us, our comercial intercourse is so ridiculously small that Americans will blush when the figures are told. M. McKenna said :

'The value of goods imported into Chili in 1864, according to official statistics, was $18,867,363; and would any of you believe that in this commerce, of which you might have as good a share as any other nation, while England is represented by forty-three per cent, the enterprising, the prosperous and active people of the United States, with their enormous and crowded and countless manufactures, stand only in the proportion of five per cent? But that is a fact, according to late official returns, and I may add, as far as my personal knowledge goes, that there exists in Valparaiso, among hundreds of large European houses of commerce, only three American firms.'

England has forty-three per cent of the trade with Chili, France has twenty per cent, Germany without a fleet, and with only a few ports, has yet nine per cent, the United States, with California and Oregon lying on the same ocean, has got only five per cent, but little more than Brazil, which has three per cent.

But if our commerce with Chili is small, it is no greater with others of the South American republics. We seem to have neglected those states, whose prosperity and progress nevertheless are of great importance to us. Under the rule of the slave-lords, our attitude towards them was made purposely hostile; the slave-holders did not care for legitimate commerce; they thought only of filbustering expeditions, of snatching the land of our neighbor republics to devote it to slavery. But with the new spirit which animates our policy, our intercourse with other American republics should largely increase, our relations must become more intimate, and we shall no doubt presently recognise our duty towards them, to guard them, by our alliance, from such wanton attacks as that of Spain upon Chili, and that of France against Mexico.

True statesmanship would bind together all the republics of America in a common brotherhood; thus only can our example have its proper influence upon our neighbors, and thus only can those weaker states be saved from the attacks of despotic European powers—attacks which are as much directed against us as against our neighbors, for they arise out of hostility to the republican institutions of which we are the upholders. Mexico no sooner begins to show signs of the triumph of order, intelligence, and constitutional forms, than Napoleon makes war on the republic, forcibly sets up a despotic emperor in place of the constitutional government, involves the Mexican people in financial ruin, interrupts industry, vastly increases the national debt, reestablishes peonage, and overturns all that had been accomplished by the adherents of lawful liberty in Mexico in a quarter of a century. So Spain wantonly attacks Chili, puts the people of the republic to the expense of defending themselves, and thus retards the industrial development of that free nation. Thus, too, she intrigues in Peru, ostensibly to "revindicate" obsolete rights and claims, while her real object is to keep that growing republic in turmoil, to foster the spirit of factions, and to overturn and destroy the beneficial results of free government. It is alike our duty and our interest to put a stop to these invasions of America by European despots."

ADDRESS DELIVERED IN PANAMA

On the origin and Character of the

WAR BETWEEN CHILI & SPAIN,

In accordance with the following Act, which we copy
from the Mercantile Chronicle of Panama,
of December 12th, 1865.

AN ACT,

In the city of Panama, on the 8th of November, 1865,
a large number of Columbians, resident in this Capital,
assembled in the porticos of the Cabildo House, for the
purpose of taking into consideration the attitude which this
country ought to assume in the contention which has
arisen between Chili and Spain ; Señores Manuel Maria
Diaz and Pablo Arosemena being named respectively President and Secretary of the meeting ; and the former having stated in a fitting and well-applauded speech the object of the reunion, the latter made the following proposi-
tions, which were unanimously approved:

1st—The Republic of Chili, in the unjust war to which
she has been provoked by the agents of Spain in the Pacific, deserves the sympathies and aid of republican America.

2d—Consequently, the persons who compose this meeting consider it an inevitable duty to aid the sacred cause
of Chili by all the lawful means within their reach.

3rd—Let a commission of three persons be named, who

3

shall take charge of setting forth the plan that ought to be adopted to secure so great an end.

By virtue of the will of the meeting, the President appointed Señores Gabriel Obarrio, Pablo Arosemena, and Mariano Arosemena to compose the said commission.

The President, on behalf of those assembled, then invited Señor Benjamin Vicuña Mackenna, who was present, to address the meeting, to which that gentleman responded in the following words, which we translate from the Spanish :

Sr. Vicuña Mackenna, said : Gentlemen, although I am in this city nothing more than a simple citizen of the Republic of Chile, I cannot do less than rise to respond to the amiable invitation of the President of this noble and patriotic meeting, and offer you my profound gratitude for the manifestation you have made in behalf of my country. I cherish the deep conviction that the generous resolutions which you have adopted will resound as an echo of fraternity in the hearts of all my countrymen, who are also yours, because, gentlemen, if in the days of peace we have the right to call ourselves friends and natural allies, in the hour of danger we are nothing less than brothers. Your noble conduct is proving this. [Cries of Yes! Yes!) I did not wish, gentlemen, to pass beyond this simple expression of my personal gratitude towards you. It was my desire to assist at this splendid reunion in the character of a mere sojourner on the Isthmus, and though it be indeed true that I have been honored by my government with an important political commission, this does not give me diplomatic character to impart a determinate importance to my words. Nevertheless, on finding myself in the midst of you, and on listening to your ovations to my country, these two questions have occured to me, which I also address to you. Why does Spain make war on Chile ? Is this war against Chile only, or is it against all America ? Why does Spain make war against Chile ? Ah! You well know, gentlemen. Spain makes war against my country because she presented herself to sustain the honor and dignity of America, without any other advice, without

any other authority than her own dignity : —(Applause)
—because she made out of the attack on the Chinchas a
personal and common honor, of immediate security, of
future independence for herself—for all the sister republics
of the New World ; because, in fine, she was the first
among them in offering herself, a noble holocaust, to a
disinterested patriotism—to an abnegation without conditions. (*True!* and vehement applause for Chile.) But
Chile, gentlemen, could not act in any other manner.
Could she break the traditions of her glorious past, which
present her as always associated with all the sacrifices and
with all the ancient American glories, in which her banner
had floated in the breeze of battle together with the banner of La Plata ; together with the banner of Peru ; together with the banner of old and glorious Columbia,
from Maipú to Pichincha ? Could Chile forget that
the moderate prestige which she has cultivated among
her sisters on the Continent she owes only to her international policy, always just and honorable, always frater-
nal in council, always disinterested in aid, always intrepid
—permit me this word of patriotic pride—always intrepid
in her undertakings in common with them ? Could Chile,
in fine, shelter herself under a cowardly silence, and hiding
her noble head—her more noble heart—as in a state of
stupid torpidity, between her sea and her mountains,
avail herself of the impunity which her natural position might seem to offer to her selfishness, and abandon
thus a brother wounded so deeply, without asking for
him and with him the reparation due ? No, Chile could
have done nothing like what would have been her disgrace, and consequently she placed herself from the first
moment on the weaker side,—on the side of the injured,
the neighbor, the brother. (Applause.) But was there
by chance in this a violation of any international right ?
Was a public motive given to Spain for complaint,
for secret grievance—pretext even, I will not say for this
war, which will always seem a madness in the eyes of
enlightened nations, but for a diplomatic rupture which is
the utmost limit to which nations, in the present condition
of public right, are accustomed to go, in manifesting their
mutual dissatisfaction ? With my hand placed upon my
heart, I declare that no public nor private act took
place in Chile that should bring upon her the animadver-

sion of Spain. There are, to respond for my veracity, those noble and patriotic notes of the cabinet of Santiago, which reduce to mere dust every fictitious circumstance of recrimination which had been raised against Chile by the mischievous emissaries of Spain. There is not in them a single charge which has not been dispelled. There is not a single accusation which has not been confronted and confounded as an error or as an imposture. There is not a single affront which has not been answered with the noble dignity of right and moderation. (Vehement acclamations of "Long live Chile"—"Long live President Perez"—"Long live the Covarrubias Ministry.") But, gentlemen, when the world pronounces as you do between Chile and Spain, it is evident that the former gains already half of the contest. I may in truth say to-day, that in the conflict between nations there are two battles to be fought. The first is the battle of right. The second is the battle of force. A day will arrive in which humanity will not have to submit save to the former of these tests, when its grievances will be decided by humanity itself; but though that hour has not yet arrived for us, its dawn announces itself with vivid brilliancy. See what has happened yesterday in Italy. See what is taking place to-day in the Great Republic of the North. See what will take place to-morrow in a republic—unhappy, but a sister, and beloved of our heart—in the republic of Mexico. (Cheers for Mexico. Cheers for Benito Juarez.) See also what will take place to-morrow in another republic, sister likewise of Mexico—sister likewise of the United States of Columbia—in the republic of Chile! (Applause.) Yes, gentlemen, Chile has already gained that first battle of right, and she has gained it not on the paper of her own chancery, but all the representatives of neutral nations, common friends of Chile and Spain—and from whom perhaps the latter believed herself to have a better right to expect a favorable decision—have declared her victory in an explicit, solemn and durable manner. There remains then only the battle of force to be decided; and I hope, gentlemen, it will be decided soon and gloriously. (Applause.) There is not in this a challenge offered to Spain. On the contrary, Chile, whose prosperity was borne on the thousand wings of progress, has not desired this war, has not provoked it, would avoid it even at this very hour at the cost of all sacrifices, with the exception of one only—that of her honor. (Vehement acclamations.) But when that war is thrust in our face by an uncivil ultimatum, selecting the grand anniversary of the country's birth for the affront, and consummating it afterwards with the scandalous pillage of our unarmed bays—what remains to be done but to accept that war and prepare ourselves for the combat? (Applause.) Yes, we have accepted it, and we will march cheerfully to encounter the common enemy, after having invested in the Ark of the country, our gold, the fruit of noble labor; and we are disposed to water her fields, which that labor had fertilized, with the best blood of our brothers. (Bravo ! Bravo !) Now, I ask, shall we fight alone while America, for whose cause we have unsheathed the sword, look passively at the struggle ? (Unanimous cries of No! No!) Or shall we renew, gentlemen, those grand days when Bolívar and San Martin breaking loose like a sublime tempest from the furthest extremities of America, discharged in the heart of those mountains which the hand of God has placed all along our boundaries as a common bulwark, the thunderbolt of Ayacucho, the thunderbolt of independence and of the liberty of America ? To you who are the sons of Bolívar and of Santander, of Sucre and of Miranda, to you who are the representatives of the three nations of Old Columbia (which heaven grant may again reunite in one reconciled family), to you it belongs to answer. (Enthusiastic acclamations—prolonged Cheers for Bolívar, San Martin, and Cochrane, etc.) And at this appropriate moment permit me to make a pause and bring forward the second question which I introduced at the beginning. Is this war only against Chile or is it against all America ? Spain has always given, as the only reason of her aggressions from Valparaiso to Panamá, the respect of her citizens violated by our people and governments, giving for their foundation the death of two country laborers in a domestic broil, I know not in what farm in the vallies of Perú. But the accusation in itself, was it just, was it true ? No, gentlemen, on the contrary, permit me to state that the accusation is based only on the most abject, iniquitous of frauds, the fraud of ingratitude. More than sufficient right has the American to detest the name of Spaniard, especially in the present century and on the present soil. I need make no comments on this,

I am treading the soil which Morillo conquered. I am
standing on the country of Caldas and of Pola Salavarrieta
(prolonged applause.) But the easy and magnanimous
heart of Americans soon forgot all this, and the Spaniards returned to find among us, I will not say an asylum but, a home, a new country. See what is taking place
in all the great cities of South America, in Carácas, in
Bogotá, in Buenos Ayres, in Quito, in Lima, in Santiago,
in Panamá itself. In all parts you will find Spaniards ad-
vantageously located in commerce, in the clergy, in public
posts, in society, at the very firesides of the Americans
who have given them fortune, family, and as much or
more happiness than would have fallen to them in
their own far off country. (It is true! It is true!)
If this be so, how dares the Spanish Government assert
so vile and ungrateful a calumny? How pretend to
exact from us that respect which of ourselves we
freely give; for, gentlemen, respect is not decreed (laughter and applause) by pointing at our breasts the mouths of
her cannon. The truth is, that Spain, as a people,
does not feel, and does not believe anything of this kind. I
know Spain. I have sat, not long since, at her firesides.
Relatives, by me beloved, live there. I feel the generous
blood of her race boil in my veins, and I esteem Spain
because I have a memory, and I cherish in my republican
heart the sentiment of justice for all. But the Spanish
government, which does not feel or believe this either, and
which makes its first victim the noble but unwary and
credulous Spanish people, fosters the imposture for its
own ends, miserable ends which Spain herself will some
day repudiate. *The violation of respect*, therefore, is nothing else than a pretext for systematic aggression —
for the war already general against America. The true
cause is, on the contrary, that which is the least respectable in the intercourse of communities, it is the *guano*.
(Applause.) And otherwise, do you believe, gentlemen,
that to pursue that chimerical respect for her subjects,
Spain would have unfolded this policy uniformly aggressive and invasive towards all those that were formerly her
colonies? Do you believe that General Gandara was sent
to the solitary and once obscure shores of unconquerable
Santo Domingo solely in search of respect? Do you believe that the valiant, the honorable General Prim took a

Spanish army to Mexico, by virtue of a tripartite treaty extorted from France and England, in coercion of that same respect which Spain—proud Spain, declared herself impotent to obtain alone? Do you believe that Admiral Pareja, the least respectful of the courteous Spanish Marine, came to this coast in search of respect in the Pacific? Do you believe that for this same respect the Commisario Mazarredo let loose on the world his famous doctrine of *revindication?* And be it understood, citizens of the United States of Columbia, be it understood that you have not yet been recognised by Spain as an independent people (several voices, "We do not wish it! We do not need it!") be it understood that neither the Narvaez Ministry, nor the O'Donnell Ministry have disapproved, as the Pacheco Ministry did in the tribune—in the tribune alone—the principle of Mazarredo: and you well know that what one Ministry in Spain does, that which succeeds undoes; and that while one Minister is sent to adjust a treaty under the faith and honor of nations, another is sent to destroy it by cannon shots. (Applause.) But permit me to continue, bringing to mind what Spain has done to force from us respect for her sons. (laughter.) Do you believe that through respect for Mazarredo, for his poisoning in a glass of beer on board the steamer *Paita,* for his assassination by the clatter of empty kerosene cans, for his persecution in a fantastic hand-car to Colon by all the colored people of the Isthmus, do you think that for all these fabulous stories Spain would send and maintain in the Pacific the most powerful squadron that has been seen in these waters, and precisely at the time that her navy emerged from its secular prostration, when she most needed it on her own coast to sustain her rank as a nation of the first order which she had solicited; when it was urgent for her to collect it on the shores of Cuba now placed in the twofold danger of a triumphant insurrection in Santo Domingo and the abolition of slavery in North America, two terrible and intrusive infections which she can ward off only with a triple sanitary cordon of iron-clad ships ? Do you believe, that Spain would send, as she did not delay in sending, new reënforcements in support of that respect, that her ships may rot in listlessness in our harbors, making herself forgetful of that traditional history already converted into a proverb among our people,

that no ship of war that ever doubled Cape Horn with
the Spanish flag has returned to view the waters of the Atlantic ? [Applause and shouts of "Viva Lord Cochrane" !] And do you believe, in fine, that she would
have claimed from Perú the payment of a prodigous
sum of millions in which are included the expenses of
the war of Independence, exacting for this outrage
the double mortgage of her honor and her revenue ?
And do you believe, finally, that only in quest of
respect Admiral Pareja exacted that Chile should burn a
little powder for the penon of her Admiral's ship, and
because she did not do so declares war against her and
treacherously seizes her ships ? Oh ! No. It is essential that this undignified farce should be concluded, for
us and for the world. It is essential that the armed hand
of America should lift up the curtain of this comedy
with which an attempt is made to deceive all nations and
Spain herself; and to declare, once for all, that the cause is
one, that the principle is common, that the danger is iden-
tical for all. For in truth, gentlemen, that which is being done is the excavation on our entire borders of one
sepulchre, in which if they thrust us one by one it is
only to render more facile the task of these royal grave-
diggers who still believe they do us an honor because,
on casting our dead bodies in the pit, they enshroud
us with their purple robes. (Bravos). And in this coming war, I should say, in this war raging this very day,
permit me to point out two distinguished points which
will have a vast influence in the development of this
contest ; *the Chincha Islands*, the sole object which Spain
covets, and *the Isthmus of Panamá*, the sole strategetic
route by which Europe can attack the Republics of the
Pacific in their vulnerable side. And do not believe
that the Chincha Islands should be always a property solely and exclusively American, because of the
treasures which they contain, but because a maratime
European Power of the first or second rank, once mis-
tress of them, could maintain in the Pacific a squadron
so powerful that it would be necessary for us to sail
out of our ports with hats in our hands to plead
permission of these new lords of this same sea which
half a century ago we made ours by force of victory. [Applause.] And will all America consent that

this shall happen ? Will England and America, apart
from every moral affection, from every notion of justice,
from every interest of the balance of power, tolerate
that their commerce shall be submitted anew to the
same laws which governed the Peninsular monopoly
in the days of the famous affairs in Portobello and Panamá ? Will they consent that Spain, whose financial ruin reaches the last extremity, — not to say
the utmost disgrace, according to the news which the
steamer that arrived this very day at Colon has brought
us,—should cancel her bankruptcy with English capital,
North American capital, the capital of all the markets of
Europe, invested on a gigantic scale in the commerce of
the Pacific ? This, gentlemen, is what we shall know
when the news arrives, from Europe and the United
States in the early days of the coming year, of the effect
which the conduct of Admiral Pareja has produced ; and
the war between Spain and Chili which, if to-day
it be an isolated aggression, will to-morrow be a continental act. But with regard to what you will do on
the Isthmus of Panamá, this route which to-day is the
property of all free and enlightened nations, but which
to-morrow may possibly be also the momentary property
of invading rulers, we need not await news from any part.
Will you consent, all the ports in the Pacific once closed,
as I deeply hope they soon will be, to the Spanish squadron, that their public or private emmisaries should take
from this Isthmus a single naval supply, a single grain of
powder, a single grain of wheat, a single grain of sand ?
(Unanimous cries of *No* ! *No* !) And if to sustain these
noble intentions you should have to fight among your
picturesque mountains, in the wild defiles of your grand
railway, against a bold invader, I am sure of this, you
will not fight alone. There will fight by your side every
man of courage who has come to reside in this city, the
centre of the universe from its furthermost extremities ;
there will fight with you the English, the German, the
Scandinavian, the Italian, and above all there will fight
with us, those sons of North America whom I perceive
here in a considerable number ; for all those men adore
in their hearts that sublime motto, the Isthmus of gold,
as eternal as the Isthmus of land on which we tread, and
which must always unite the two Continents of America

in one single group, in one single family, in one single home—the Doctrine of Monroe—*America for the Americans!* (Enthusiastic and prolonged applause. Long live Chile and America.)

Dr Pablo Arosemena was next called for, who made a few pertinent remarks in the same strain, which were interrupted by frequent applause. The meeting then adjourned until the commission shall again convoke it for their report.

LETTER OF

B. VICUÑA MACKENNA,

To the Editor of "La Epoca," of Madrid,

UPON THE REAL CAUSES AND MOTIVES OF

THE WAR BETWEEN CHILI AND SPAIN.

———————

"On board the steamer Pacific, in the latitude of
Panamá, November 4, 1865.

"MY DEAR SIR—It would hardly be possible for you
to comprehend the sudden and deplorable war which has
sprung up between Chili and Spain if a frank voice from
these far-distant zones were not to explain to your just
mind and enlightened patriotism so unexpected and extraordinary an event. However, not because unknown
and humble do I refrain from assuring you that that voice
is the voice of an honest man, and a sincere friend of the
Spanish people, in the midst of whom I was so fortunate
as to pass some of the happiest days of my life. The
manner in which I am going to have the honor of addressing you will be the strongest proof of the noble motives
which prompt me to write to you these few words, which,
although hurriedly written, refer to the gravest affair with
which true Spaniards and true Americans can occupy
themselves to-day.

"After forty years of peace and independence, South
America had become thoroughly reconciled to the old
mother country. Chili had signed a treaty of peace with
her, and that country—model of loyalty, prudence, and
energy—offered to Spaniards the most unlimited and cordial hospitality. You may assure yourself, beyond a doubt,
that there is not a single Spaniard settled in Chili who
may not have made a fortune more or less considerable,

and there is not a single one who may not have Chilian children. I do not purpose to cite special cases. Inform yourself of any honest Spaniard whatever who may have visited our shores, and if that man does not wilfully distort the truth, I am not afraid for a single moment of being falsified. On the contrary, Chili, on account of her mild climate, her productions similar to those of the Peninsula, the serious character of her people, her traditions of order and respect for the laws, had become the favorite resort of those who came from Spain to these regions in search of a home and a new country.

"How is it, then, that all this has disappeared in an instant, and, according to the latest dates (Oct. 17), Admiral Pareja should be in Valparaiso, threatening that rich and splendid city, and that there should be collected in Santiago, under the vigilance of the police, all the Spaniards, to serve as hostages for the consequences of an attack, otherwise unpunished, against her defenceless people.

"It is that which the Lima periodical I have the honor to enclose will explain to you, in the article entitled "Fortnightly Review," and which I will try to make clearer in a few words.

"Since the announcement of the coming of Admiral Pinzon, there has been in Chili and in Perú a vague rumor of alarm. The aggressive tendencies of Marshal O'Donnell were well known, and the annexation of Santo Domingo —the first threat against American nationalities—was recent. The personal conduct of the Admiral, and the arrival of Commissary Mazarredo converted that rumor into a suspicion. The military occupation of the Chinchas, and the famous declaration of recovery, unfortunately gave cause for those doubts and fears, and converted them into an international scandal.

"The aggression of Admiral Pinzon was against Perú, but Chili could not be indifferent. Her geographical and commercial position, her history, her security, were all involved in that question. Picture to yourself Portugal invaded by France, declaring the right of conquest, or any other offense aginst her nationality. Could the Government of Spain, without being guilty of treason and mibecility, remain indifferent, simply because the attack was not directed against her own territory?

"A better comparison can not be made, for it was exactly what took place. You know that, in 1820, San Martin had come from Chili to liberate Perú, because the independence of that country was the complement of ours. You also know that, in 1830, another Chilian army defeated General Santa Cruz, President of Bolivia, who annexed Perú to that country, and that, also, because the safety of Perú was our own safety.

"But how did Chili manifest her adhesion to the cause of Perú? That is the only question to be solved, because in it are found all the *claims* which have given rise to the war. The people, by acts purely evidences of sympathy and enthusiasm; the Government, by no act which was not in entire conformity with the law of nations. I know how much has been falsely attributed to the country and to the Government in this matter, but the notes of our Chancery and the Tavira-Covarrubias settlement, are ample proofs of what I assert. I will make yet another observation. When the war in Mexico commenced against the Emperor of the French, collections of money were made throughout the country, and large sums were sent to President Juarez, to enable him to maintain the independence of the country against the French invaders. Could a case be shown of more evident hostility against France? What was the satisfaction demanded by the powerful and susceptible Government of Napoleon III.? None whatever. And that because the governments of Europe, in spite of the dense cloud of error and calumny which darkens our republics in their eyes, understand that we are subject to the same impressions, the same alarms, the same sympathies which are felt by the people whom they govern, and consequently subject to the same duties and the same obligations. And in this light permit me to ask you, would Russia have declared war or demanded satisfaction for the public manifestations, the contributions of money, the popular processions, the simultaneous and persistent attacks of the Press in France and Spain in favor of unfortunate Poland? Why, then, should the popular sympathy of Chili for a brother and neighboring country, violently assaulted and offended in her honor and the principle of independence which was common to us, be looked upon in any other light? You should judge the affairs of America as the affairs of all civilized countries ought to be judged;

then, and only then, will you enter the regions of reason, of mutual advantages, of civilization itself.

"But it has been said that there was a real insult to the Spanish flag, and that the name of Isabel II. was dragged through the mire of defamation ; and these two imputations have been made a *question of honor*—an immediate and sufficient cause of war. It may be just for me to assure you, on the faith of a man of honor and truth, that the first assertion is entirely false. I was a present witness of the event of the 1st of May, 1864, and there was not even the slightest affront to a flag then still friendly, and which was placed, as usual, on a staff so elevated, that no one could have touched it, though desirous of doing so.

"With regard to the second charge, I must acknowledge that there were mean and cowardly acts on the part of an obscure paper, gotten up for speculation upon the scandal of an exceptional situation. But did not the Government protest against this journal, offering to try it according to the laws ? Did not society protest and condemn it to scorn ? What more could one wish that it should have done ? And in Spain itself have not journals of high grade been published, offensive to the throne—as the *El Guirriga; y El Tío Camorra*, among others ? What wonder, then, that the *San Martin* should come to light in an aggrieved and justly-distrustful country ? And the *Punch* of London, and the *Charivari* of Paris, do they not publish pictures and articles highly offensive to the dignity of the Spanish monarchs ? And will Spain, because of that, demand satisfaction with the mouth of the cannon, and declare war against those countries ?

"In reality, there has been no offense against Spanish honor which should give occasion for war, still less justify it. If the Spaniards have always been treated with cordiality and kindness ; if they have all found fortunes, family, and social considerations like the native sons of the country, and with even a preference over strangers of other nationalities ; if in forty years of peace, there has never been a single mutual quarrel between the two countries— no shadow—not a single diplomatic rupture whatever ; if the treaty of peace in force for more than twenty years has never been violated ; if many of the highest employees of the Government, in the Republic, and even in her Consular Corps, are Spaniards, how, then, can the object of the war be the obtaining of satisfaction from Chili, so generous and hospitable, or reparation for offences which have never been committed ? How can they make a pretence of vindicating Castilian honor which has never been offended, and which, on the contrary, has been respected in all that really demands respect ? Truly, either the Spanish Government is wilfully blind, or her agents have put a traitorous bandage over their eyes ; because, by the war which she has undertaken, she will reap only calamity and disaster, instead of the benefits which a long and honorable peace have furnished.

" I ask again, how is it that this war exists, and threatens the two countries who are engaged in it with injuries without end ?

" I do not wish in this place to discuss the events with which the Press in Spain and America has already occupied itself, and which have brought things to that deplorable state in which they are to be found, and which have been judged according to their real value, which amounts to nothing after discarding Pinzon's boasts and Mazarredo's fears.

" I will only permit myself to show you how, in relation to Chili, there has risen from such slight causes, so insignificant, so accidental some of them, so *entirely free* of bad intentions, and so unworthy, all of them, of occupying for more than an hour the attention of two civilized countries—a tumult of recriminations which have dragged us into a war lamentable for both.

" I am going to place before you, with the sincerity of a righteous mind, the truth—the sad, but stern truth—of all that has happened. I fulfill thus the principal object of this letter, and conform with the promise which I made at the commencement, to explain the almost fabulous events which are unfolding themselves in the Pacific.

" Unfortunately for Spain and Chili, there existed in the latter country a diplomatic agent of the former, whose character—generous, but without energy or judgment—was found subject to the influence of any one, and easily prevailed upon to take any particular course. Señor Tavira, with whose personal friendship I have been honored, had these defects among his numerous good qualities, and consequently he was involved in disgrace.

"In the first days of the Chincha troubles, there arose, as was natural, a violent party among the Spaniards resident in Santiago. This was principally composed of three doctors—two of some merit, and a homœopathist who, we know not why, has had bestowed upon him the Cross of Charles III, which to-day he would have deserved to lose, on account of his contemptible adulation to the Chilians since war was declared. These men made themselves the head of a party, and united night after night in gatherings, at the house of a bookseller, also a Catalan, who should have had nought but feelings of gratitude and respect towards a country in which he counted many friends, and in which he had made his fortune.

"By that circle, and through the means of accomplices, Señor Tavira was urged to get up claims, to raise charges, to invent accusations to blow the flame between the two countries, these leaders forming a party, by means of letters written to Spain, combinations with the Spanish squadron then lying off the Chinchas, and an active propagation among the Spaniards of all classes, not only in Chili, but in all the republics of the Pacific, and even those of the Plata. This was the more incomprehensible in the leaders of this agitation in Chili, inasmuch as all of them were married to Chilians, and had children in the country. Now they wander scattered, and anathematized as ingrates, to a country to which they have done innumerable wrongs, in return for its having given them wives, homes, and respect.

"Moved by these strong but unworthy influences, Mr. Tavira qualified the position which Chili took in the Peruvian-Spanish question in a way completely false, exaggerated, and odious. And permit me to make known here, that if the Spanish Government had not possessed aught but the notes of her Minister, and the perfidious private communications which had been written to Madrid from the Pacific, in demand of crosses or lucre, by which to judge of what had passed, she would not have formed an opinion different from that which she has manifested, nor have followed a line of conduct different from that which she has followed. But since, joined to these accusations and claims—sometimes puerile, sometimes senseless, and always unfounded—there have gone to Spain the replies of our Chancellor, it was necessary to be wilfully blind in order not to see, overthrown and confuted, all those imputations. So certain is this, that Mr. Tavira himself, turning from his first impressions, formed through the opinions of others, and hidden intrigues, voluntarily called the convention which bears his name, and whose violent condemnation neither in Chili nor any country of the globe could be understood or explained, because in it the question of mutual honor was settled beyond all susceptibility.— Thus at least they made haste to declare it, for the justification of Chili in Spain, to all the Cabinets of which was given official knowledge of that settlement.

Upon this point, I may be allowed to make an earnest protest against one of the basest calumnies which have been forged by bad Spaniards against the dignity of Chili, and Spain herself. I allude to the senseless but widely circulated rumor, that M. Tavira had received a heavy sum of money to make the referred to settlement. Such a charge is beneath discussion. Spain has not such vile sons as would sell her honor for gold, nor is Chili so mean-spirited as to seek peace by bribery. There was, in truth, an incident, traitorously distorted, which might have given rise to that imposture. When, on the first of June of the present year, Deputy Matta, objecting to the paragraphs of courtesy in the Annual Message of the President of the Republic to the Spanish Government and to her Minister in Chili, as an excessive condescention, said, in his discourse, "that perhaps these manifestations were the fruit of a *secret understanding* between the Spanish Envoy and the Chilian Chancery." But that *secret understanding* about the phrases of a public document could never be interpreted as a suspicion or an allusion to base fraud. It is also said now, by the public voice of those countries, that the partisans of the war are interested in the negociation of the heavy debt which Spain claimed from Peru, and that that is the cause of her aggression upon Chili, and of her policy resolutely hostile to America. But be it said, in honor of the race to which we all belong, such calumnies are only worthy of the obscure adventurers who invented them for a speculation. The humblest politician in Chili would be above such an imputation, and we have no reason to believe that such is not the case in Spain.

Thus I have briefly treated, but with chivalrous fidel-

3

ity, the true history of the first part of this affair, otherwise almost incomprehensible. It appears that there were intrigues on the part of the discontented and violent who created, by means of the unwary spirit of the Spanish Minister, an imaginary diplomatic quarrel, and the storm, which afterwards increased by evil winds, by the agency of unsettled and ambitious characters in the Spanish squadron, by innumerable manifestoes indiscriminately signed, by the pure spirit of companion and countrymanship (and probably by motives less noble) has become a positive war between two countries which yesterday were living in the most perfect harmony.

Now permit to me consider the second part of this lamentable affair, or rather its denouement, for it is almost impossible to imagine that causes so insignificant should have produced such disastrous results, unless in this same denouement there may have intervened circumstances equally peculiar and no less incomprehensible to a dispassionate critic, than those which I have hastily mentioned.

In this unfortunate conflict, all has been a question of words. As, at the commencement, the bland and indecisive disposition of Mr. Tavira gave origin to the difficulty, so, in the end, the persistent obstinacy of Admiral Pareja has provoked the war. He was the most active promoter of the dissatisfaction with the Tavira-Covarrubias settlement, and since his arrival on the shores of the Pacific—where he was born—has manifested such an inimical spirit to Chili, that many have been led to believe that he was prompted in his actions by the singular idea of avenging the death of his relative, General Pareja, who fell in the War of Independence, commanding a Spanish army on our coasts, fifty years ago.

The Tavira settlement, disapproved by the Spanish Government, through the influence of her Admiral in the Pacific, and Tavira himself dismissed from office, the error was committed of urging to the utmost reparation for the offence given and of replacing the Minister who was responsible for it. This was a signal evidence that Spain herself intentionally *sought* a war with Chili. The same thing had been done in Peru respecting the assault of Pinzon. Mazarredo was sent to make right his misdeeds, and, entrusted with the curing of the disease, had only made it worse. It was desirable to put an end to the difficulties caused by the Tavira Convention, and so Admiral Pareja was sent to Chili—the very man who had been its bitterest censor, and who was interested in condeming it under all its phases. Could this fail to kindle the flame which threatens to embrace us all, if the wood or the fire are approached to the pile already prepared ?

And not only that ; as an individual, as a character, Admiral Pareja has done all that was in his power to make a settlement impossible. He chose the glorious day which we celebrate as the anniversary of our independence, to arrive in our ports, without any intimation whatever tending to reunite the diplomatic relations which had not yet been broken, he sent us a peremptory and offensive ultimatum, to which there was no reply except war, and in fact commenced this by establishing, with four men-of-war, a blockade over the seventy or more ports of our coasts, without any previous notice to neutral comcommerce ; seizing all Chilian property within reach of his guns, and jesting at all positive law of the public right of nations, as has been made evident by the unanimous protests of the Diplomatic and Consular Corps accredited to the Republic.

Thus it has been not events, but characters, not the offences of one nation against another, but the isolated acts of individuals, not mutual advantage nor the demands of the law of nations, but the personal defects of the emissaries of Spain, which have brought about this sad conflict, whose consequences it is given to none to foresee. The weakness of Mr. Tavira in getting up accusations destitute of all foundation, and the violence of Admiral Pareja in aggravating them by unjustifiable acts—in them you have the only cause of this war of individuals, of imperfect organizations, of inconsiderate elections on the part of the Spanish Government, so far, unfortunately for her, from the theater of events, and consequently incapable of comprehending their true character.

And it is necessary, sir, that you should understand that I speak here under the hypothesis, honorable and rational, that all Spain seeks in Chili is reparation for an imaginary grievance, and that such a claim may have been made in the most complete good faith.

I ought to declare to you, with the moderation which I

have tried not to lose for a single instant throughout this communication, that if unfortunately, Spain should cherish views with regard to our moral and forced submission to her influence, or of aggression upon our territory, or of isolated pretensions or in combination with other European powers, whichever they may be, and which have a tendency to alter in the least our institutions, Spain and her allies would have but one thing to hope for, now and always, from all Chileans—war, unceasing war, until the entire Republic were a mountain of ruin and her people *en masse* an immense cemetery.

Judge these events dispassionately, Mr. Editor, bringing to bear the public documents which refer to them, and this brief review of the private, or, if you will, mysterious part of them, and putting your hand upon your heart—the heart of a loyal and honorable Spaniard—declare if there is any cause, pretext or excuse whatever, for this war between two nations of the same origin, the same associations, and the same religion.

In the meantime, it is not for me to say what Chili will do in this contest, to which, without any desire or fault of hers, she has been provoked.

I will only permit myself, before concluding, to simply ask—having made evident the fact that this war ought not to be—that it is without justification or possible excuse—*what is the object* which Spain has in view in carrying it on ?

I understand that there may be, even in this age, wars without cause or motive, and with no other foundation than the abuse of power. But although I understand that, Mr. Editor, I cannot possibly imagine the existence, in these times, of a war *without an object.*

What does Spain pretend ? Does she covet conquests, mercantile franchises, influences, political or purely social like those which England proposes to wrest from Japan with the canon, and Spain and France united from Cochin-China ? No ! Nothing like that has the Spanish Government in view, because in truth it would be to insult her deeply to suppose that by such means she should propose to accomplish those ends in the present stage of civilization and the law of nations. Spain, then, rendering full homage to her good faith, simply proposes the *revindication of her honor and the respect of her subjects in those distant countries.*

I have already clearly shown that that honor has not been offended in the least, and that that respect to Spanish subjects has been accorded in Chili, not from fear of Spain, certainly, but from innate love towards her, to the utmost limits of the most generous hospitality.

But I am willing to admit, for a moment, that Chili was guilty of one or the other fault. Was the course pursued by Pinzon, Mazarredo and Pareja the one which ought to lead to a satisfactory solution of the difficulty—to secure the noble ends which the Cabinet of Madrid had in view? Certainly not. On the contrary, the very opposite to that which they claimed should have been the result. Facts are proving it.

Mr. Tavira, in threatening notes, asked *explanations* from our Government, showing, in support of his haughtiness, the mouths of the cannons of his fleet. Nevertheless, the Chilian Government, without descending from its dignity, neither in its actions nor in its language, satisfied these diplomatic exactions fully and under the faith of the Spanish Government itself, through her exacting envoy.

These explanations cast aside as insufficient, Admiral Pareja, instead of demanding others more satisfactory, as he appears to have been authorized to do by his *ostensible* powers, (explanations which Chili could still have given, without injury to her honor), sent an *ultimatum*, which is the last word of nations before the voice of the cannon. Did she succeed thus in her object? Quite the contrary, as you well know.

Subsequently, he declared a *blockade* of all our ports, as a means of pressure. Has he progressed thus in his plans? The declaration of war was our reply.

And, now, what more can he do? *Bombard* our ports, as he vaguely insinuates in his last dispatch to the English Minister in Chili. But in case of such barbarity, would he have the right to condemn the inevitable reprisal on our part?

Will Spain send new ships? Will she send troops for disembarkation? Will she drain her treasury and her best blood in expeditions much more distant than those of Santo Domingo? And in the meantime, Chili, who needs assistance from no one to enable her to live and fight, will maintain her ground to a man, and the object of the war will never be attained.

Behold then, Mr. Editor—a war *impossible* of success on account of its causes, which had hardly authorized a diplomatic rupture, and which is going to be *impossible* in the attainment of its object.

And with regard to the *weakness of Chili*, for which you yourself, Mr. Editor, have asked, within my remembrance—doubtless, with the best intentions—a "little compassion," permit me to say a word, which will certainly not be a boast.

There is one force relative, and another intrinsic, possessed by all nations. Of the former, all the advantages are in favor of Chill, on account of the distance, the stormy seas, the high price of provisions, the scarcity of spoil in her waters, all the prerogatives, in fact, natural to a country which carries on a war in her own territory against one which comes to attack her from a distance of three thousand leagues.

But Chili certainly relies more upon herself, upon her intrinsic strength than upon these accidents, which to a certain extent are extraneous.

She relies upon her credit intact, and which stands highest in the markets of Europe. She relies upon the homogeneousness of her race and the political unity of all her inhabitants. She relies upon the valor always shown by her sons, upon those facile means which maritime law sanctions, and by which the weakest people may carry destruction and ruin to the very heart of the strongest. She relies upon the indomitable patriotism of her sons, who, in fifty years, have raised themselves from the most miserable colony of Spain to the most flourishing Republic of that part of the New World ; and lastly, upon the justice of her cause, recognized, in the most explicit manner, solemnly and unanimously, by the impartial representatives of all the countries mutually friendly to Spain and Chill, and perhaps more friendly to the former than to the latter.

Judge, then, Mr. Editor, if Admiral Pareja is likely to succeed in the object of this war, which he alone has brought about, and which he alone expects to bring to an end by the right of might.

Do you know how that Republic has replied to the threat of war which Pareja has intimated with his four ships ? By ordering the prolongation of telegraph lines

throughout the Republic, the opening of immense high-
ways, the completion of four or six lines of railroad in
actual construction, the abolition of all taxes, and above
all, by unanimously rejecting in Congress, (where the writer
held an honorable place,) a law confiscating the property of
Spaniards, at the very moment when the Spanish ships
were confiscating all the Chilian property which they found
within their reach.

Let the Spanish nation reflect upon what is passing in
those distant seas—let the Government open its eyes to
the light, the clear light of facts, and not to the obscure
and false light of mysterious acts and deceptive intrigues
—and she will see that if a profound and immediate
change does not take place in her policy towards these
people, an immense abyss opens before her future. This
is not a threat, Mr. Editor. Heaven grant it may not be
sad prophecy !

In the meantime, I have fulfilled, to the best of my
ability, the promise which I made to you at the beginning of this letter—to speak only the truth of this deplorable affair.

To you and your colleagues of the press, who have done
rare but honorable justice to our people, it is given to
judge them as you see fit, inasmuch as I do not impose
these revelations upon you, although faithful and well-
meant, as a rule of conduct, nor upon the press, nor upon
the people of the Spanish Government.

With sentiments of distinguished consideration, your
most obedient servant,

BENJAMIN VICUÑA MACKENNA.

THE MONROE DOCTRINE.

GRAND MEETING IN THE COOPER INSTITUTE,

JANUARY 6, 1866.

IN DEFENCE OF THE REPUBLICS OF

Chili, Peru, Mexico and Saint Domingo.

From the New York Times of January 7, 1866.

Quite a large meeting, all things considered, was held last night in the large hall of the Cooper Institute, for the avowed purpose of reaffirming the spirit of the Monroe Doctrine, and of expressing a sympathy with the feebler and struggling Republics of the Continent. The hall was appropriately decorated with bunting and transparencies. On a strip of cloth, stretched across the front of the platform, were the words, "Heroic Santo Domingo, Chili, Peru, Mexico. If they have not conquered, they will conquer." And on a draped transparency, the words, "Henry Winter Davis. His spirit lives with us to-night."

At eight o'clock, Mr. Squier, accompanied by W. C. Bryant, Peter Cooper, Edward E. Dunbar, Hon. Mr. Paston, and others, entered the hall, and were greeted with cheers.

Mr. Squier called the meeting to order, read the call, and nominated Mr. Bryant as President, with Messrs. Webb, Garrison, Jerome, Beekman, Cooper, Tieman, Leavitt, Walker, Greeley, Dunbar, Rosecrans, Paston, &c., as vice-presidents, and Messrs. Bell, Wheeler, and Anthon as Secretaries.

President—William Cullen Bryant. *Vice-Presidents*—William H. Webb ; Cornelius K. Garrison ; Leonard W. Jerome ; Hon. James W. Beekman ; Peter Cooper ; Danl. F. Tieman ; Rev. Joshua Leavitt ; Hon. Robt. J. Walker; Major-General J. A. Garfield ; Manton Marble ; Hon. Horace Greeley ; John E. Williams ; Edward E. Dunbar ; Major-General Rosecrans ; Hon. Hiram Walbridge ; Hon. Theo. E. Tomlinson ; General E. L. Viele ; Hon. Charles D. Paston. *Secretaries*—J. B. Wheelock ; Col. J. W. Watson ; Col. A. H. Duganne ; Jas. L. Anthony ; Joseph Bell.

SPEECH OF WILLIAM CULLEN BRYANT.

FELLOW-CITIZENS : I cannot better state the purpose for which we have come together than it has been stated in the call and in the observations made by the gentleman of the committee who has just addressed you. We are here, as he very truly said, not for the purpose of creating public opinion, but of giving it a free, a full and enthusiastic expression. We have come here to assure the Government of our support in resisting such audacious attempts as we have lately seen to interfere in the politics of Mexico. (Applause.) It is with deep sorrow, my friends, that I find myself unable to introduce to you this evening one whom we expected to make the principal address here, Hon. Henry Winter Davis, of Maryland. He was engaged to be present, but death interposed between him and the fulfilment of the engagement, and that eloquent voice, to which you would have listened with so much pleasure, that voice which always spoke from a full mind, and which uttered the dictates of a sincere, manly, generous, and fearless heart, is silent forever. To Winter Davis, more than to any other man in Maryland, that State owes it that she choose the better part, and remained among the States that were faithful to the Union.— (Applause.) If he had lived, he would have added to the obligations to him under which his country now rests, by maintaining and vindicating with all his eloquence and all the enthusiasm of his noble nature the cause which has called us together to-night.

Mr. Bryant then announced that it was the intention of the committee, after the reading of the resolutions and letters, to adjourn the meeting to some other evening, when the attendance of prominent men, now detained by business in Washington, could be secured.

Mr. Squier then read the following letters:

FROM HON. MONTGOMERY BLAIR, LATE POSTMASTER-GENERAL.

WASHINGTON, Dec. 12, 1865.

To the Committee of the " Monroe Doctrine" Meeting, New York.

GENTLEMEN: I regret that my professional engagements prevent me from accepting your invitation to participate in your meeting. The recent concerted aggressions of European powers on the free States of this Continent, culminating in the outrage of Spain upon Chili, demand an outspoken expression of American feeling. The President in his recent Message has declared, in the calm and dispassionate tone becoming the gravity of the occasion and the dignity of his place, that these wrongs must cease.— Our people should now meet and manifest their purpose to sustain him in upholding Republicanism in America. I rejoice that the people of New York intend to respond so promptly.

The late rebellion was the work of these European Powers. By their money and intrigue it was inaugurated. They fomented, encouraged, and recognized it, with a view to suppress the growth of republicanism in Europe, and to resume their sway over this continent. We should, in my opinion, have sooner crushed the rebellion if we had boldly from the first confronted the instigators of it, and afforded the lovers of freedom in Europe an opportunity to help us, by striking at our enemies there. Shall we take longer counsel of an unreasoning dread of these Powers, and continue to tolerate their aggressions, which have cost us so dearly; or shall we imitate the wiser boldness of our fathers, whose manly courage saved our country and our sister republics from such wrongs, even whilst we were comparatively a feeble Power? Are those European tyrants so strong in the affections of their own people or in material resources that we must bow before them, and speak with bated breath of the right of the American people to be exempt from European conquest? Far from it. It is because we have sapped the foundations

of their thrones in the hearts of their people that they
have conspired against us ; and they have conspired only
because they dared not offend their own people by striking
us openly.

The people of France are still loyal to the traditions
which allied them in feeling and in arms with our own
people in the last century. They are as indignant almost
as our own people at the blow thrust at us through Mexico by their Emperor. It is not the waste of their means
or of their blood which makes the Mexican enterprise so
odious to the people of France ; it is the proof it affords
that the third Napoleon is false to the policy and to the
friends of that Napoleon whose name was his passport to
the throne, and that he is doing the work of the allied
despots who dethroned the great Napoleon, in seeking to
destroy free government in America, which the founder of
his dynasty aided in building up and strengthening as' a
bulwark of the freedom and power of France. No gen-
uine Bonapartist can think the honor of France committed
to the maintenance of a Hapsburg on an American throne.
On the contrary, they feel dishonored by the attempt, and
by the cruel and unjust war waged by the Emperor upon a
distant and unoffending people to consummate it ; and
we shall but respond to the liberal and enlightened feeling
of the French nation by remonstrating against it, and even
by a resort to force, if that shall be necessary, to check
the Emperor in his mad career in Mexico. The historian
of the Empire assured them, from his place in the French
Assembly, that we would do this when we had suppressed
the Southern rebellion ; and the liberals of France will
rejoice, as we do, that the first Message of the President,
after that event, makes it certain that they will not be dis-
appointed.

I am, gentlemen, very respectfully,
Your obedient servant,
MONTGOMERY BLAIR.

———

FROM SENATOR NESMITH, OF OREGON.

UNITED STATES SENATE CHAMBER,
WASHINGTON, Dec. 27, 1865.

HON. E. G. SQUIER, *Chairman, &c.*

SIR : I have received the communication of your committee of the 20th instant, inclosing a call for a meeting at the Cooper Institute, New York, on the 6th proximo, having in view the public expression of sentiments upon the subject of "Foreign interference in the domestic affairs of this continent." In reply thereto, I regret to say that public duties in this city will prevent my compliance with the invitation with which you have honored me to be personally present.

I have much gratification, however, in saying to you that the purport of your meeting has my earnest sympathy and support. I can see no objection to the public agitation of a subject that has become, by recent events, so deeply interesting to the people and government of our country; and, on the contrary, I believe in the abundant cause and the appropriate occasion for announcing our opposition to any assaults upon, or interference with, the integrity of public institutions on this side of the Atlantic.

I have always been impressed with the correctness and propriety of the political theory enunciated in the annual Message of the President of the United States on the 2d of December, 1823, in allusion to this subject; and I am convinced that what was then uttered by President Monroe as pregnant with consequences, near and remote, to affect the interests of our country, has increased force in its application now. The eventful history of our country for the past four years should certainly give claim to a recognition from the nations of the earth of ability to preserve our institutions; and the success and prosperity in every civilized attribute of great nationality that has marked our onward course since the foundation of our government, surely entitles us to national pride and the right of rank in the class of great nations. After the overthrow of Bonaparte, the four great monarchies of Europe (and I believe, in the early stages, England, too, favored the alliance) formed what was known as the "Holy Alliance," whose object was to extend their principles, and oppress and put down popular institutions. Have we any less claim as a great nation, and interested in the promulgation of our theory of Government, to strengthen, aid, and support our sister republics near us? Does not our own interest, perhaps safety, demand positive hostility to any attempt to break down free government near us?

I regard the attacks of Spain upon the South American

States as futile and unimportant. From the time of that nation's first attempt to reclaim her American possessions to the present, every effort in that direction has been a failure. The hostility of Spain alone to either Perú or Chili can, in my judgment, never be very formidable.

It is the other nation mentioned in your communication whose present condition invites my warmest sympathies, and excites my indignation at what I have always regarded as an outrage upon her people, and a covert attack upon our government. No reasonable claim ever existed to warrant the seizure of the Mexican Republic by the Emperor of the French. No just cause for war demanded the invasion of her soil. None of the rights of property gave the semblance of a title to the possession of that country. Mexico, disturbed by internal dissensions, and weak, was seized upon through the promptings of avarice and by the strong arm of power; and a ruler and a form of government repugnant to the very large proportion of her inhabitants was forced upon the country. An empire was created by force of arms with a people eminently republican in their notions of government. An emperor was placed over them who was, in every sense, a foreigner, without the most remote claim, by either association, language, or consanguinity, to be their monarch.

While the energies of our own government were directed to the suppression of the most gigantic rebellion the world ever saw, the Emperor of the French stole into Mexico, in a clandestine manner, and usurped the government. He selected the only period of time when he would have dared to perpetrate an outrage from which resulted great aid and assistance to those intent upon the destruction of Republican government in our own country, and practically became their ally. We have, happily, subdued the rebels at home; and the troops who consummated that result should not have been disbanded until the co-laborer in that rebellion and his mercenaries were driven from the soil of our sister Republic.

In conclusion, I have to state that I am earnestly in favor of our government reasserting the Monroe Doctrine, and, if need be, vindicating it at the mouth of the cannon.

I am very, respectfully,

Your obedient servant,

J. W. NESMITH, of Oregon.

FROM HON. JOHN CONNESS, UNITED STATES SENATOR
FROM CALIFORNIA.

SENATE CHAMBER, Washington, Dec. 12, 1865.

DEAR SIR: Your note inviting me to attend a meeting to be held in New York, for the purpose of giving expression to American opinion on the subject of the " Monroe Doctrine," is just received.

It will not be in my power to be present on the occasion ; but I can assure you fully of my concurrence in the movement.

No more opportune time could be selected for a protest of the American people against the interference of European monarchists with republican institutions on this continent than the present.

The constant menace of the baser tyrannies of the old world during the recent rebellion will remain fresh in the memories of our people for many a day. The advantage taken by the Emperor of France of our direst troubles and needs in the invasion of Mexico, and the attempts of that usurper and traitor to liberty to establish an empire there by force of arms, has no parallel in history. Undertaken by him upon the double pretence of a defence of French interests, and in behalf of " order," he has become the author of wrong and disorder, which must continue until he shall withdraw his hirelings and pretenders to the place whence they came.

Spain, following the bad example, has assaulted the Republic of Perú, and exacted terms which the people of that noble country have contemptuously rejected. Upon the most shallow and baseless excuses and allegations, Spain has followed up her attack upon Perú by an assault upon the independence of Chili, which republic was menaced by war, or presented the alternative of degradation. To the everlasting credit of that gallant, free, and peaceful people, the guage of war has been accepted, and now it is for a just world, but particularly for the American people, to decide whether these constant interferences and assaults on republican institutions and the public peace shall continue. For one, I am in favor of plain language to European Powers. We are for peace and good will on earth. We do not claim the right of forcible propagation of our political principles ; but we believe in them and in the advantage to mankind of their extension.

You shall not suppress them by force. You have not been appointed by the world as masters, neither as pacificators according to your practice. We speak in our own behalf, and in behalf of the independence of nations and peoples.

Let this be our diplomacy, not diluted until dissolved, and my opinion is that we will soon enter upon an era in which the practice of each nation of the world will be to mind their own business.

I have the honor to be, your obedient servant,
JOHN CONNESS.

To Hon. E. G. Squier, Chairman, &c.

FROM HON. ROBERT DALE OWEN, OF INDIANA.

NEW YORK, Jan. 1, 1866.

GENTLEMEN : Your kind invitation finds my time so engrossed that I am unable to prepare anything worth giving to the public at your meeting next Saturday.

I take a deep interest, however, in the subject. It is not now a theory of which we may safely put off the solution for years. It knocks at the door. It involves the fate of our nearest neighbor.

I do not regard the twenty-year-long dissensions of Mexico as the mere result of individual ambitions, or as the national brawls of a people incapable of self-government. I see in these the great struggle through which all nations must pass—the contest between privilege and oppression on the one hand, and liberal principles and institutions on the other. They had their incubus as well as we. Ours was slavery ; theirs the overshadowing temporal power of a church which held in fee one-fourth—some estimate, one-third—of all lands and houses in the Republic.

Like us, they brought their contest of long years to a successful termination. Like us, they might look forward, as the reward of victory, to a prosperous and peaceful future.

Their hopes were blasted by foreign interference. The excuse was that they must be governed by others since they could not govern themselves. But despotism is not the remedy for internal commotions ; least of all, despotism in America under European protection.

National peace is, of all national blessings, the greatest. Therefore, it behoves us to avoid not only the immediate but the more remote causes of war. I do not believe that we can maintain permanent peace with a European despotism next door to us ; but neither do I think that war will ensue, in this case, if resolution, with good temper, mark our policy now.

We must be bold in the present, if we would avoid war in the future. The " Monroe Doctrine," temperately asserted, is peace.

I am, gentlemen, your obedient servant,

ROBERT DALE OWEN.

To the Hon. E. Geo. Squier and others, Committee :

FROM HON. DANIEL S. DICKENSON, OF NEW YORK.

OFFICE DISTRICT-ATTORNEY OF THE U. S. }
FOR THE SOUTHERN DISTRICT OF NEW YORK. }

NEW YORK, Jan. 5, 1866.

GENTLEMEN : Your note inviting me to address a meeting at the Cooper Institute to-morrow evening, called to indicate the popular sentiment on the subject of the " Monroe Doctrine," has been received, and my thanks are returned for the complimentary remembrance.

There is, perhaps, no question of national policy, either foreign or domestic, upon which the American people of all sections and parties are so firmly united and so resolutely determined, as upon that of resistance to the encroachments of monarchy upon this continent. In short, so often and so unanimously has this sentiment been asserted and repeated that the world knows it by heart.

The world knows, too, that it is one of the most cherished principles of republican institutions ; that it is deemed essential to their safety and exemption from the conflicts which are wont to spring up and flourish in the pestilent atmosphere of monarchy ; and the world *should* know, that it is the last point to be yielded to force or be circumvented by fraud.

Entertaining, as I do to their fullest extent, these convictions, I am aware that the subject is at this time somewhat interwoven with our foreign relations, always a delicate subject, and especially so at this time, when we are surrounded by jealousies and irritations ; and having full confidence in the wisdom and patriotism of the President, his Cabinet and Congress in the premises, I have deemed it proper, in view of an official relation with the Federal Government, not to mingle in popular demonstrations upon the subject at this time, lest such action might be misconstrued or misunderstood to the prejudice of others

I have the honor to be, gentlemen,

Your obedient servant,

D. S. DICKINSON.

Hon. E. Geo. Squier and others, Committee.

FROM HON. R. T. VAN HORN, OF MISSOURI.

WASHINGTON, D. C., Jan. 4, 1866.

GENTLEMEN : I have delayed an answer to your invitation to attend a meeting on the 6th with the hope that it would be possible to be present, but I am compelled to forego that pleasure.

Let me say a word. The air is full of strange rumors, which are well calculated to alarm every patriotic American. We must appeal to the people at once, and arouse the country to the danger.

If a monarchy be established in Mexico, we shall be untrue to our duty, and will receive the execrations of the lovers of Freedom throughout the world.

The talk that Napoleon will withdraw his troops, if let alone, may be true ; but they will be withdrawn when the liberties of the Mexican people shall have been trampled under his feet.

There is but one way to secure their withdrawal—and that is, the open, manly one, of a notice to quit, backed by a demonstration on the frontier to enforce it if declined.

The great West is ready—it is a unit, and will not be silenced.

Illinois, Missouri, Iowa, Kansas and Colorado will drive out the foreign troops, without a man being taken from other States.

5

All they are waiting for is the word, and they will answer for the result.

₁Very respectfully, your obedient servant,
R. T. VAN HORN.

Messrs. E. GEO. SQUIER, E. L. VIELE, CHARLES D. PASTON, A. H. DUGANNE, J. A. WHEELOCK, Committee.

FROM HON. J. BAKER, OF ILLINOIS.

WASHINGTON, Dec. 21, 1865.

Hon. E. G. Squier and others, Commmittee :

GENTLEMEN : My duties here as a member of Congress will preclude my attending the meeting on the 8th of next month, to which you invite me. I will add, however, a few words on the particular subject which you have in hand.

The present French Emperor has somewhere said, in substance, that one of the Napoleonic ideas is, to keep step with the movement of one's age ; and that if a man fails to do this, by standing still or going backwards, he is apt to get run over—a first-rate idea, by the way—but the Mexican scheme of the Emperor is a flat violation of it. The idea will prove itself true in this as in hundreds of other instances ; the scheme will fail. The movement of the age is progressive, not retrograde, or even stationary. The tendency is to larger liberty, in fact, in form, and among *all men*, and will not allow the founding of a throne, at the point of foreign bayonets, upon the ruins of an American Republic. The idea of being flanked by such a monarchy upon our southwestern border, presided over by an offshoot of the House of Hapsburg, is perfectly preposterous, and not for a moment to be entertained by any friend of liberty in America or Europe. The thing is morally, politically, historically impossible, and never would have entered the head of Louis Napoleon, had he not been entrapped, by his want of sympathy with freedom, into the shallow supposition that this country was going to be done for by the rebellion. In my judgment, this Republic should stand for liberty on the continent, and firmly protest against any further foreign coercion of the political system of Mexico.

Yours, very respectfully,

J. BAKER.

FROM HON. CHARLES SITGREAVES, OF NEW-JERSEY.

PHILLIPSBURG, N. J., Dec. 27, 1865.

Hon. E. G. Squier and others, Committee :

GENTLEMEN : I regret that previous engagements will prevent my attendance at the meeting to be held in the great hall of the Cooper Institute, in New York, on the evening of Jan. 6, for the purpose of giving expression to the sentiments of the people on the subject of the Monroe Doctrine.

Although " absent in body, I will be present with you in spirit." This Continent must be, in all its length and breadth, the home of constitutional freedom and the asylum of the oppressed of every land, which it never can be with an empire on its borders.

Our people must never add to the oceans of human blood which have been shed and mountains of treasure that have been expended to "maintain the balance of power," which they must do if "foreign, and especially monarchical, interference is permitted in the domestic and international affairs of this continent." You say truly, that the time is appropriate for an expression of opinion on this subject. It is, indeed, appropriate, not only for the reiteration, but for the maintenance and enforcement of the " Monroe Doctrine." The stability of the Union, the future tranquillity of the nation, the extension of republican principles and the rights of man, alike demand it. Now is the proper time. The opportunity now lost can never be regained, without destroying the peace of the world. An earnest declaration by Congress and the President now, I think, would be sufficient ; but if not, then a million of brave men, disciplined in the march, the camp, and the battles of a four years' sanguinary war, will, under God, settle the question of despots for ever.

Very truly yours,

CHAS. SITGREAVES.

FROM. MAJ.-GEN. J. A. GARFIELD, M. C., FROM OHIO.

HOUSE OF REPRESENTATIVES, ⎱
WASHINGTON CITY, Dec. 26, 1865. ⎰

HON. E. GEO. SQUIER:

DEAR SIR : Yours, inviting me to address a meeting at the Cooper Institute, on the application of the Monroe Doctrine to our relations with Mexico, Perù and Chili, is received. I regret that my duties here will not allow me to accept your invitation. I should be glad to cooperate with you in an effort to inform the citizens of my country by what means and for what ends the monarchies of Europe have been, and are still, endeavoring to trample out republican liberty in the New World. I trust you will call the attention of the assembly, that will meet on Saturday evening, to the fact that Maximilian, the French agent in Mexico, by a decree of Sept. 5, 1865, re-established slavery, with a view to encouraging emigration from our rebel States ; thus affording another proof that the French usurpation in Mexico was in reality a part of the rebellion, for the purpose of extending and perpetuating the institution of slavery.

I believe that a firm and decided course on our part will, without war, secure the removal of the French usurpation. That the usurpation will cease, and the pretensions of Maximilian and Napoleon in Mexico will be relinquished, I have no doubt.

I am, dear sir, very respectfully yours.

J. A. GARFIELD.

———

FROM HON. B. F. WADE, U. S. SENATOR FROM OHIO.

WASHINGTON, Wednesday, Dec. 27, 1865.

HON. E. G. SQUIER :

SIR : I have just received your note inviting me to attend a meeting to be held in the City of New York, on Saturday evening next, " for the purpose of giving expression to the sentiments of the people of New York, on the subject of foreign, and especially monarchical, interference in the domestic and international affairs of this continent." I regret that I shall not be able to be present at your meeting, but you may be assured that I am heartily in sympathy with the declared object thereof, and intend to make my sentiments known in Congress at an early period of the present session.

I have the honor to be yours, &c.,

B. F. WADE.

FROM MAJ.-GEN. SICKLES.

CHARLESTON, S. C.
[Extract.]

I regret that my duties here, and the reserve imposed upon me by the regulations of the military service, prevent my participation in a public demonstration, having for its noble object the expression of the sympathy of the people of this country with Chili in her struggle with Spain, and of the unfaltering adhesion of the United States to the Monroe Doctrine. But my co-operation will not be missed, for our people are unanimous and immovable in their sentiments of attachment for our republican sisters of the American Continent : and although we are weary of war, European powers will not be wise in assuming that we lack either the means or the inclination to repel aggression.

DANIEL E. SICKLES.

FROM HON. JOHN A. KASSON, OF IOWA.

HOUSE OF REPRESENTATIVES,
WASHINGTON, Dec. 21, 1865.

Hon. E. G. Squier and others, Committee :

GENTLEMEN : Your note of the 20th instant, announcing a meeting at the Cooper Institute on the 6th proximo, to give expression to the public sentiment on the question of European interference with American Republican institutions, and requesting my attendance, is received.

It will afford me sincere gratification to be present if it shall be possible. The occasion has come for the Great Republic to acknowledge its assertion of the "Monroe

Doctrine" to have been an empty phrase, or a pregnant principle of Republican, national and continental safety, to be enforced with the whole combined power of the American Republics if required.

Let our counsels be prudent, as our preparation should be complete. Let the reaction from Europe, treacherously begun in the hour of our distress, itself have reasonable time to react in view of the increased solidity of the United States at the close of our war.

Then, if justice, honor and respect for American principles do not retract the interference already initiated by Europe, let the blows fall, in the name of God and Liberty, until the interfering flags shall have been swept from the two oceans that embrace our continent.

I am, gentlemen, your obedient servant,

JOHN A. KASSON.

FROM HON. SCHUYLER COLFAX, SPEAKER OF THE HOUSE OF REPRESENTATIVES.

WASHINGTON, D. C., Dec. 21, 1865.

GENTLEMEN : It will be impossible for me to be present at your meeting in New York on the 6th of January ; but, while trusting that our country may not become involved in hostilities with any foreign nation, if they can be honorably averted, I have no hesitation in expressing my warmest sympathies with the struggling and unconquered Liberals of Mexico, and my faith that both President and Congress will so act and speak, that the whole world will understand and appreciate the deep interest we feel in the permanency, the tranquilization, and the consequent prosperity of our neighboring Republic.

Yours truly,

SCHUYLER COLFAX.

FROM HON. HAMILTON WARD, OF NEW YORK.

WASHINGTON, D. C., Dec. 21, 1865.

To Hon. E. Geo. Squier and others, Committee :

GENTLEMEN : I am in receipt of yours of the 20th, inviting me to attend a meeting at Cooper Institute, New

York City, on the evening of Jan. 6, in vindication of the "Monroe Doctrine."

Circumstances will not permit my attending, as it would give me great pleasure to do. I hope there will be a grand outpouring of the people on that occasion. Give the "Nephew of his Uncle" to understand that as the great Napoleon at last found his Waterloo, he too may find his in the Halls of the Montezumas.

The French ruler took advantage of our supposed weakness, and planted upon this continent, over our unwilling people, a monarchy, in bold defiance of our well-known and cherished national policy and traditions. However much we might desire peace with our old friend across the water, this act of France places us in the position either to fight it out, if needs be, and vindicate our policy, or tamely submit to a great national insult and wrong. The people are of but one opinion, that the national honor must be maintained. Let them speak out.

, Respectfully yours,
HAMILTON WARD.

FROM HON. R. W. CLARKE.

WASHINGTON CITY, Dec. 21, 1865.

Hon. E. GEO. SQUIER, *Chairman, &c. :*

SIR : I have received your notice of a call for a meeting to be held Jan. 6, 1866, at the great hall of the Cooper Institute, New York, "*for the vindication of the Monroe Doctrine.*" My arrangements will not permit of my attending your meeting; but be assured that if called upon to act officially upon that question, I shall be with you most heartily.

Respectfully,
R. W. CLARKE.

FROM HON. HORACE MAYNARD, OF TENNESSEE

WASHINGTON, Dec. 21, 1865.

GENTLEMEN : Your invitation to be present at a meeting in the Cooper Institute, on the 6th of January next, finds me on the eve of returning to Tennessee. The object of the meeting, to give expression to the general, nay, universal, public sentiment, popularly known as the "Monroe Doctrine," meets my unqualified approval. Let the sentiment find expression on every convenient occasion, and through every practicable medium.

It has been assailed on both continents of the Western hemisphere, and it is high time it were authoritatively asserted.

Very respectfully,

HORACE MAYNARD.

Hon. E. G. Squier, *Chairman.*

FROM HON. SAMUEL J. RANDALL, OF PENNSYLVANIA.

PHILADELPHIA, Jan. 1, 1866.

Messrs. Squier, Viele, Poston, Duganne and Wheelock, Committee, etc. :

GENTLEMEN: Your invitation to be present and address a public meeting in New York City, on the 6th of January next, called for the purpose of vindicating the Monroe Doctrine, has been received.

I regret that my official duties will prevent its acceptance.

I have always supported the doctrine you wish to maintain, and have so voted in Congress. I am prepared to use all constitutional means to carry it into practical force and effect, and assume any responsibility which may arise therefrom.

I am, gentlemen, your obt. servant,

SAMUEL J. RANDALL.

FROM. HON. JAMES H. LANE, U. S. SENATOR FROM KANSAS.

WASHINGTON, Wednesday, Dec. 25, 1865.

GENTLEMEN : Your valued favor was duly received ; and in answer, I regret to say previous engagements will prevent me from attending. This I much regret, as I am on the record as an advocate of a firm and decided policy

in regard to resisting the great conspiracy of imperialism
to overthrow our republican form of government on this
continent. And it would give me more than usual pleasure, in such a presence as that of a New York audience,
to denounce the foreign despots who dared first to seduce
part of our people from the path of duty, and then, in
the midst of our national troubles, to plant their iron heel
on the neck of our feeble and distressed sister Republic,
Mexico. You may rely on me in every contingency in
the future for peace or war.

Respectfully,

J. H. LANE.

LETTER FROM MAJ.-GEN. MUSSEY.

WASHINGTON, D. C., Jan. 5, 1866.

Hon. E. GEO. SQUIER &c., *New York.*

MY DEAR SIR : I am very reluctantly compelled at
this last moment to decline your invitation to attend the
meeting at Cooper Institute to-morrow.

I regret this the more as I am thoroughly in sympathy
with what I understand to be the object of the meeting, a
public declaration, to wit: of the American belief that
the New World is for Republics, and that it is the duty
of the United States to enunciate and maintain this
belief.

Since the triumphant success of the United States in
the late rebellion, republicanism is no longer an open
question.

The Revolutionary War showed that a Republic could
assert itself against a Monarchy and acquire independence ; the war of 1812 showed that it could maintain
that independence as against outsiders ; the late war has
shown that it can maintain it as against the turbulence
and sedition of the malcontents of its own citizens, aided
by the moral and material sympathy of allied France and
England. And to every thinker the demonstration is
overwhelming that a " People's Government" is the most
beneficent in Peace, the most powerful in War, and the
most secure against Treason.

This success has brought its duty with it for us to perform, and it is a duty which we cannot honorably neglect or evade.

We must assert the truth we have proved, must defend it when assailed, and encourage it when of feeble growth.

" This should be our Foreign policy." Anything else misrepresents us and dishonors us. If necessary, we should maintain this belief with arms. But I do not think any nation is foolish enough to court war with us, and our request will, in nearly every case be tantamount to a command, and when we do command we shall be obeyed.

For no monarchy can afford to go to war with a Republic, demanding the recognition of republic principles —since our national success has weakened every throne and strengthened every democratic yearning of the masses, upon whom thrones are built. And though kings and parliaments may order war, it is the people who carry the muskets and pay the taxes, and the people of no monarchy that could engage in war with us would submit to the burdens of a war against their and our cause.

If we are true to ourselves we shall have no wars upon this account. The moral sympathy of the Government and the material aid of our citizens, united, will give to us peace, and to republicanism all the support it needs.

Believe me very truly your friend,

R. D. MUSSEY,

Major-General.

Mr. Squire then read the following resolutions :

RESOLUTIONS.

Whereas, It was early declared, with a solemnity becoming the enunciation of a great principle, by a President of the United States, whose title to immortality and the gratitude of mankind was secured by its annunciation, that the American Continents, by the free and independent positions which they had assumed and maintained, were thenceforward not to be considered as subjects for future colonization by any European Power, and that any attempt by European Powers to " extend their system to any portion of this hemisphere would be considered as dangerous to our peace and safety ; and *Whereas,* it was equally declared that any interposition by any European Power, for the purpose of oppressing the Republics of America, whose independence the United States had, with great consideration and just principles, acknowleged, or for the purpose of, in any way, controling their destinies, would be viewed as the manifestations of an unfriendly disposition toward the United States ; and *Whereas*, in open contempt of the principles thus early laid down, France has interfered to oppress our sister Republic of Mexico and to control its destiny against the choice of its people; and *Whereas*, Spain has interfered to extend her system over Hayti, and is now interfering to oppress the Republics of Chili and Peru; therefore,

Resolved, That the United States is bound, by her traditions, by every consideration of honor and dignity, by her plighted faith to the Republics of America, for the sake of her safety, peace, prosperity and rehown, to vindicate the great principles enunciated by Munroe, in all parts of this continent, and to establish, if necessary, by force of arms, that America belongs to Americans, and is consecrated to republican institutions.

Resolved, That by the promulgation of the " Monroe Doctrine," and its constant indorsement, we have assumed a responsibility towards our sister republics, and an obligation to defend and protect them which it would be cowardly and dishonorable to neglect or repudiate.

Resolved, That we deplore with heartfelt sorrow the sudden death of that accomplished statesman and noble and eloquent champion of republican freedom and human progress, Hon. Henry Winter Davis, of Maryland, who had engaged to speak to us to-night; and we here reassert the language and sentiments of the resolution carried by him unanimously through the House of Representatives, in the Winter of 1864: "The United States are unwilling by their silence to leave the nations of the world under the impression that they are indifferent spectators of the deplorable events now transpiring in the republic of Mexico, and that they therefore think fit to declare that it does not accord with the policy of the United States to acknowledge any monarchical government erected on the ruins of any republican government in America under the auspices of any European Power."

REMARKS OF MR. TOMLINSON.

Mr. Tomlinson, after alluding briefly to the death of Mr. Davis, traced the progress of Republicanism from the West to the East, and showed in terms of bitterness the conduct of Europe and the continent toward the United States during her recent struggle. I regret, said he, that the grave has taken one who could enlighten you on these matters, but I am glad that the first meeting in the advancement of this great cause is held in this metropolis. History shows us that on all great questions great men are timid. Cabinet ministers and high officials wait till the common people speak, and then are ever glad to ride them. It's the picket who first meets the shock of battle, and it may be a proud hour for you, that you are here in the first of this movement when few distinguished men are present to address you. I want to say a few words on international law. There is no such thing as international law, because there is no arbiter of law. The conscience of the people is the arbiter. Who was it that expressed the international law when the Collossus of the East, Russia, stretched its hand to take the sick man Turkey from his bed ? The express messengers were Campbell and Pellissier, and our express messengers to Maximilian will be McClellan, Grant and Sherman. [Applause.] Now we hear that our Secretary of State has gone on a voyage to the South, and probably will say to Maximilian, the thousand things that would not look well on paper, for diplomacy, you know, is not always that which can be put on record. It won't do for us to permit the planting of any monarchy on our shores. There are monarchists enough among us now who despise our institutions, and would gladly hail any attempt to institute such a government here. In regard to the Fenian question, I will not discuss its propriety or impulses : the latter are right. But if I could say anything to Great Britain, I should say, beware, beware. If you encourage France to establish a monarchy in Mexico, the green flag of Ireland shall float above the Irish shore. [Applause. A voice—" Oh, nonsinse."]

Mr. Squier then read the following resolutions :

Resolved, That the Republic of Chili, by her dignity, firmness, and courage, as well as by her moderation and the justice of her cause, in her contest with Spain, provoked by an attack as groundless as mercenary, deserves the respect and sympathy of all free countries, and especially of the United States, with which she is identified by community of institutions and by every consideration of interest, and whose gratitude she merits as a warm and devoted friend of the American Union in the hour of its greatest peril.

Resolved, That we admire the spirit and enterprise of the little navy of Chili, and rejoice in the brilliant success which has crowned its endeavors in its contest with the arrogant flotilla of Spain.

Resolved, That the glorious example of Santo Domingo and the final triumph of the heroism and patience of her sons, should sustain and encourage the American republics in their struggles against foreign aggression.

REMARKS OF B. VICUÑA MACKENNA.

CITIZENS OF THE UNITED STATES.—I offer you my sincere thanks for the manner in which you have received the resolutions which have been presented to you in favor of my country. Your kind sympathies, your enthusiastic applause, show that you have comprehended the true position of Chili in her quarrel with Spain. I entertain the hope, therefore, that you will adopt those resolutions, as an act of justice due to a country who knows how to fight for her honor and her liberty. (Applause.)

But permit me to address you, not as a man occupying a public position, of any nature whatever, but as one of the many members of the great community of those who love liberty, republicanism, and democracy.

And in that character, it is right that I should tell you that there, in that far away but noble land, in which I was born, your country is admired and loved, as you admire and love it; that there we learn in our mothers' laps to repeat, with profound reverence, the name of the father of your institutions, the name of George Washington—(applause); that there, also, the young mothers of to-day teach their children in the cradle to pronounce and bless the name of the greatest redeemer that ages have seen since our Saviour—the name of Abraham Lincoln, of sacred and glorious memory. (Prolonged applause.)

But at the same time, let me also tell you, that beyond your southern frontiers there exists another America, sister to yours, unknown and forgotten by you, but which, if not so happy or so powerful as your country, is as worthy of your esteem and respect as any civilized nation of the globe whatever.

You well know, gentlemen, that calumny, ignorance, and, more than all, the secret intrigues of European Courts, and of their emissaries, have combined to misrepresent the existence of democracy in South America, and to nourish in her bosom the desolating struggle which is harassing her republics, without exhausting or exposing them to death.

Besides, it is necessary that each race should suffer for its original sins, and work out its own salvation. You had in the robust heart of your country the seed of Africa, and when you considered yourselves most secure in the support of your institutions, of your peace, and your progress, there broke loose upon you such a gigantic rebellion as the world had never seen.

Another such has happened to us. We had in our bosom the seed of Spain—the country of Europe which is nearest to Africa (applause and laughter)—and therefore we have struggled for half a century to exterminate the roots of ignorance, of fanaticism, and of pride, and to build upon their ruins the foundation of a republic. You have never done us that justice of comparison according to history and truth. You were taught by your own nature, by your customs, and by the spirit of liberty and of consciousness which your forefathers brought to the Rock of Plymouth, and therefore have been able to establish and extend your powerful republic, your invading and irresistible democracy. But who were our teachers in the difficult science of self-government? They were, gentlemen, those haughty conquerors who only lived to cut one another's throats, whose only delight was in the tumult of battle, and who, instead of giving to all who were born, or to all who came among them, the plough of William Penn, put in their hands the fratricidal sword of the Pizarros and of Hernan Cortes.

But, notwithstanding that recent and bloody struggle of the republics of the South, what does it prove, except their powerful and inextinguishable vitality?

Behold, gentlemen, that which has just taken place, and you will be convinced.

There existed in the midst of the Atlantic an island almost obscure and forgotten, which ancient feuds had exhausted. Spain, always blind and always greedy, believed it dead, and suddenly and traitorously surrounded it with a double circle of bayonets and cannon. And what followed? The obscure islanders rose like heroes, ancient feuds were forgotten, and the hateful flag of Spain, after having been dragged in the mire, was driven from the country by a handful of brave men, before the surprised world. (Applause.)

It was afterwards thought necessary to organise a triple alliance for the invasion of Mexico, in spite of the internal feuds which had exhausted it. But the canon of the 5th of May was enough to dissolve this plot ; and to-day, after years of triumphs and defeats, and when the usurper boasted of having pacified the land which rejected him by blood and fire, the noise of the cannon is still heard upon the banks of the Rio Grande, as an echo of those which resounded in the Wilderness and at Atlanta.

And farther away, in Peru, where one single apostate sold his country for a little guano and a little gold, you will find a people rising against the traitor and the shame—driving out the former with ignominy, and showing themselves ready again to combat for honor and right.

And with respect to Chili. . . . But permit me to refrain from speaking of my country, and let me only point out to you, upon that flag suspended over our heads, that solitary star, which shines out so brilliantly from the blue which surrounds it. That star, gentlemen, is the emblem of Chili ; that flag is the flag of my country—the same flag which, not long ago, floating in the breeze of victory, upon the mast of a small boat, was carried by brave hands within sight of the powerful squadron of the invaders, and there, almost within reach of their cannons, made the proud Castilians lower the standard of Isabel II. (Wild applause, the greater part of the audience rising to their feet, waving their hats and handkerchiefs for several minutes, shouting vivas and hurrahs for Chili.)

And still, gentlemen, remember that we won our independence by our own efforts, without the aid of any one. (Applause.) Remember that all Europe opposed our emancipation, and we won it notwithstanding. Remember that you yourselves had, by the side of your standard on the field of battle, the colors of France and Spain, while we had only our own national ensign, and all others were enemies. (Applause.) Remember, also, that alone we have maintained that independence for forty years; and, while Spain during the present century, has appealed three times to a stranger to sustain her own institutions—to Wellington, in 1808 ; to Angouleme, in 1823; to Sir De Lacy Evans and the English legion, in 1834—we have maintained the respect of our enemies, without submitting ourselves to the humiliation of seekers of foreign intervention.

And do you know why we have succeeded in all this ? Because we also, gentlemen, have a Monroe Doctrine of our own. But it is not such a Monroe Doctrine as you have been proud of for forty years ; to be sustained beneath the illuminated vault of this brilliant hall; to be talked of by great orators, or by the voice of the daily Press—but a practical doctrine, real, to be supported by acts, by treaties, by alliances, and which, unlike you, we have always defended with our blood and our swords. (Applause.)

And Chili, gentlemen, my country, I am proud to say is the republic of the South which has put itself at the head of this grand and generous movement of brotherhood in glory and sacrifice. It was Chili who sent aboard of one of her men-of-war a diplomatic agent to the shores of Central America, to arrest the filibuster Walker. It was Chili who defeated the expedition of Cristina and Flores against Ecuador, in 1846; and who, years afterwards, tore down the altar and the mask of the French Protectorate in that unfortunate country. It was Chili who sent her gold to Mexico, and her blood to Perú. It was Chili, I do not hesitate to say, with all the frankness of which I am capable, who put herself in opposition to the plans of an administration of this republic, which perhaps you have forgotten, but not forgiven yet, and which purposed to establish a spurious American protectorate over Ecuador, on condition of the cession of the Galápagos Islands for the sum of $3,000,000.

And Chili was perfectly right, because, in the opinion of the people of South America, the Monroe Doctrine does not mean conquest without right, invasion without justice; does not mean aught but respect for nationalities which God has created, or their institutions, without any consideration whatever for those who intend to attack them, or for those who intend to protect them.

Yes, gentlemen, the Monroe Doctrine, as we understand it, is a vital and absolute principle, not a passing interest of policy. It is not a question of geography, involved in that popular quotation, *America for Americans.* It is not a question of frontiers and territories, by which this or that State may extend itself at the expense of another. It is, on the contrary, the foundation of international right in America ; and in that I differ entirely with the eloquent orator who has preceded me, because Republican and Democratic America has a theory of her own about existence and extension, just as the monarchies of Europe have their doctrines of equilibrium and of dignities, and the foundation of that theory is the Monroe Doctrine.

This principle is not, then, simply our own, but that which its glorious founder, James Monroe, meant it to be; and that which his noble sustainer of to-day, Andrew Johnson, has clearly implied he means it to be ; that is to say, that the monarchical Governments of Europe will not be permitted to interfere with republican institutions in the New World.

Gentlemen, that Power which created the strip of land which unites the two continents of America in one single world, one day inspired a great man of the North with this theory of general salvation. That day the key of the golden problem of democracy was discovered, the monarchs of Europe trembled upon their falling thrones, the freemen of the New world showed the slaves of the Old where the sacred ark ought to rest after the flood, and over the sky of a new cycle, and beyond the clouds, the hands of Washington and Bolivar clasped over the struggle of general emancipation, united the two worlds in one, to form a kingdom of eternal glory and eternal liberty.

Let that doctrine of redemption, gentlemen, be sustained, let it be propagated, let it be vindicated. Let your men of the government, or your men of war on the field of battle, carry out this work of redemption. Let the voice of Rome be heard once more from the dome of your high Capitol, and

6

thus, like the household word of Abraham Lincoln, which was—*Justice and liberty for the oppressed,* may the household word of Andrew Johnson be—*Justice and liberty for the aggressed.*

Señor Mackenna concluded his address amid a perfect storm of applause.

Mr. Squier then read the following resolution:

Resolved, That in Andrew Johnson, President of the United States, we recognise a statesman and patriot, a noble illustration of the fostering influence of republican institutions, a man of the people, deeply sympathizing with oppressed humanity at home and abroad, and who will, with firmness, prudence, and dignity, and in case of ultimate resort with all of his energies as a man and as President, dedicate himself to the vindication of those great national principles enunciated by our fathers as essential to our peace and safety, and among which the "Monroe Doctrine" is one of the most vital, and at this moment of first and practical importance.

SPEECH OF S. S. COX.

Mr. S. S. Cox was then introduced, and spoke long and tenderly of Mr. Winter Davis, with whom he served in the last Congress. The Monroe Doctrine has never yet been backed by the force of this great republic; sooner or later the force of this people will be evoked in the enunciation of the doctrine. We should not forget that the people of all these little republics are waiting anxiously for our movement. I trust the first thing to be done, after Mr. Seward is convinced he cannot write Maximilian out of Mexico, will be the convocation of another Congress of Republics at Panamá, including the Republic of Cuba, and that there the great nations of Europe may receive a lesson. Our unfortunate troubles came North and South, and Europe crept in, sneaked in by a triple alliance, and backed up this Archduke of the hated house of Hapsburg, tyrants of a hundred years. This thing will all be settled in time. I know that if we had taken decided steps in time, this trouble would have been settled ere this. Had we taken the advice of Ministers McLane and Corwin, the troubles would not have happened. Now, thank God, our own troubles are ended. Thirty millions of people reunited, as I trust and believe we are united, can do a great deal. We can put an army of a million of men into the field, and know how to use them when there. (Applause.) But I rose simply to say a few words about my friend and co-laborer, Davis, who cannot, as he hoped, be with you here to-night; and heartily sharing with you the appreciation of his noble nature, I thank you for your kind and patient attention, and retire.

The meeting was then adjourned, subject to the call of he Chair

BANQUET

REPRESENTATIVES OF THE PRESS OF NEW YORK,

AND TO THE

Members of the Diplomatic Corps of South America

RESIDENT IN THIS CITY.

———

On Wednesday the sixth of December, there took place in the splendid "Salon Bleu" of "Delmonico's" restaurant, the sumptuous banquet with which the confidential agent of Chile in the United States, Don Benjamin Vicuña Mackenna, entertained the most notable journalists of New York and the members of the Diplomatic Corps of South America resident there.

The saloon in which the banquet took place was elegantly adorned with the flags of Chili, the United States and Perú.

The seat of honor at the table was occupied by Señor Vicuña Mackenna. At his right sat Señor Bruzual, the Minister of Venezuela in the United States, and at his left the Minister of the Argentine Republic, Don Domingo F. Sarmiento. At the opposite end sat George Squier, Esq., ex-Minister of the United States to Central America, and on either side of him the Señores Navarro, Consul General of Mexico, and Fleury, Secretary of the Brazilian Legation. There assisted besides at the Banquet, as representatives of the various States of the South American Republics, the greater part of those who are accredited to the United States, and who reside accidentally or permanently in New York.

Among them were noted as representatives of Mexico, the Señores Navarro, General Sanchez Ochoa, and Señor Baz, ex-Governor of Mexico. As representatives of Cuba, Señor Santacilia, the celebrated poet and Cuban statesman, son-in-law of President Juarez, and Señor Don Juan Manuel Macias. Santo Domingo was represented by Sr. Dr. Bazora, *Chargé d'Affaires* of that Republic in the U. States ; Venezuela by her Minister to Washington, Señor Bruzual, and by the Consul-General of the same Republic, Don Simon Camacho, nephew of the liberator Bolivar ; Brazil by the Secretary of the Brazilian Legation at Washington, Señor Fleury ; Perú by the confidential agent of that Republic, Sr. Don Mariano Alvarez ; the Argentine Republic, by Señor Sarmiento ; and lastly Chili, by the Señores Vicuña Mackenna, Aldunate, and her Consul in New York, Dr. Rodgers.

Among the most notable Journalists of New York, we will notice Mr. Wilkes, the editor of various journals published in this city, and a gentleman of distinguished ability and social position ; Buckingham Smith, Esq., Frank Leslie, Esq., and Mr. Starr, Editor of that part of the *Herald* devoted to South American affairs.

There were present, also, among other distinguished citizens of the United States, the Hon. E. George Squier, late Minister of the United States to Central America, Dr. Mackay, Sub-Secretary in the Cabinet at Washington, charged with the diplomatic relations of the United States in the Spanish-American Republics, Messrs. Fabri, Italian Bankers and Agents of the Italian Government, Mr. Chauncey, of the firm of Fabri & Chauncey, Mr. Plumb, the well-known writer upon Mexico, and other gentlemen no less distinguished.

The dinner commenced at half-past six P.M. The table was sumptuous, and the service left nothing to be desired. Mr. Delmonico displayed once more the resources of his art, and that exquisite taste which has given to his establishment the reputation of being the first restaurant of New York.

After an hour of lively conversation, devoted, as was natural, to testimonials to the exquisite flavor of the viands, Mr. Squier gave the first toast, proposing a general glass in honor of Señor Vicuña Mackenna, who presided over the table. In reply, Señor Vicuña Mackenna proposed a toast in honor of the Press of the United States. He said that although in other countries, in the present condition of the human race, the press was a power, in the United States it had attained the character of a true public institution, without which the Republic could not exist; that in his opinion, the press had done more to put down the rebellion in the South than the armies of the North, in that while they were sometimes defeated and destroyed, the press had never been conquered. In conclusion, he recalled the observation of Miguel Chevalier, who by himself alone characterized the role of the press of this country. It is known that in his travels through the United States, wherever he saw a village (to-day a city,) that even where there were only three houses, one of them was a bank, the other a school, and the third a printing-office.

Mr. Wilkes, as the Deacon of the Journalists present, replied to the toast of Señor Vicuña Mackenna, asking a unanimous glass to be drank standing, to "Heroic Chili." Three hurrahs resounded at the termination of the enthusiastic toast of Mr. Wilkes. The next toast was given by Señor Bruzual who, in a patriotic speech, happily developed the idea that the American Republics, free since the war for their independence, ought to strengthen themselves by breaking the only ties which bind them to Spain —preoccupation and inattention to other ideas than those which the Revolution had given birth to, thus destroying for ever European influence in America.

Señor Sarmiento, alluding to the previous toast, said that the Republic of the United States, like a colossal iron-clad, was sailing towards the future, and that the Republics of South America, taking advantage of the tranquil wake which she leaves, will follow closely.

Señor Bazora gave a succinct account of the war of Santo Domingo and Spain, and after showing that the Dominicans had only calculated upon their heroism to combat with an army strong and full of resources, concluded, expressing his conviction that Chili would do as much, and would know how to put an end to the pretensions of Spain.

Señor Santacilia drank the next toast, that Cuba would soon add to the number of American Republics, thus assuming the position destined for her by nature, topography, history and race.

Señor Macias—That the solitary star of Cuba, darkened to-day by the cloud of slavery, will soon shine, illuminated by the splendor of that of Chili.

In continuation, Señor Baz gave the toast in honor of Mexico—as a people who, after a triple invasion, continued to combat their enemy with firmness and energy, surrounding him in their strong places ; and in honor of Juarez as the guiding star. The toast was received with enthusiasm and drank standing.

Messrs. Rodgers, Mackie, Evans, and Squier drank in turn to Chili, her hospitality, her progress, and the noble and dignified conduct observed in the present question with Spain.

Mr. Squier proposed a toast in honor of General Prim, that great, sagacious man, he said, who had foreseen the events of which America was going to be the theatre, and in accordance with the nobleness of his character, had hastened to retire from the scene.

Lastly, Señor Vicuña Mackenna gave a toast in honor of Italy and Garibaldi. He remembered that that nation was, through her democratic sentiments, the sincere friend of America, and cited Garibaldi as the only European able to represent in himself, to the New and Old World, one who had fought for the liberty of both. This last toast was replied to by Mr. Fabri in a manner as brief as eloquent, and the hour being already advanced, the guests repaired to the saloon, where coffee and liquors were served, remaining in pleasant conversation until 12 o'clock, at which hour they departed.

In allusion to this Banquet, the " Herald" says on the following morning :—

" Last Wednesday evening, Señor Vicuña Mackenna, Special Envoy from the Republic of Chili to the United States, entertained various distinguished persons from South America and the representatives of the press of New York, with a splendid dinner at " Delmonico's" restaurant, in Fifth Avenue.

" Among the guests were—Señor Bruzual, the Minister of Venezuela; Señor Navarro, Consul-General of Mexico; General Sanchez Ochoa ; Señor Baz, Governor of Mexico ; Dr. Basora, of Santo Domingo ; Señor Alvarez, Confidential Agent of Perú ; Señor Santacilia ; Señor Fleury, Secretary of the Brazilian Legation ; Dr. Rodgers, the Chilian Consul in New York ; Mr. Squier, ex-Minister of the United States to Central America ; Dr. Mackie, formerly employed in the Department of State at Washington ; George Wilkes, Esq., Frank Leslie, Esq., and the representatives of the Herald.

" The dining-room was decorated with the flags of the United States, Chili, and Peru, gracefully arranged at either end of the table. Delmonico, the prince of restaurateurs, displayed all the taste and exquisite skill of his art.

"In reply to the various particular toasts of the guests, Señor Vicuña Mackenna, Messrs. Squier and Wilkes, Señores Bruzual, Mackie, Navarro, and others, pronounced eloquent speeches. The principal theme of the remarks of those gentlemen was a strong protest against foreign intervention in the affairs of America, especially with relation to Chili and Mexico—"Europe for Europeans," and the base of all the sentiments expressed was a desire that the Monroe Doctrine should be strictly maintained, from the Rio Grande to Cape Horn. The enthusiasm and eloquence of the guests kept the party together until nearly midnight."

UNION LEAGUE CLUB.

REMARKS OF B. VICUÑA MACKENNA

ON THE

Telegraph of South America.

On Thursday evening, 6th December, the New York Union League Club held its regular monthly meeting, and after P. McD. Collins, Enterpriser of the Telegraph round the World, had delivered his address, already known to the public, the Hon. Vicuña Mackenna, from Chili, who accidentally was among the numerous guests, was introduced by Mr. Blunt, one of the vice-presidents of the Club, as a representative of the heroic Republic of Chili, who so bravely maintained her rights against old and proud Spain —a cause dear to all the American people. (Great applause.) Mr. Blunt further remarked that England had come forward to the support of Chili for the same reason that she supported the rebellion—for copper. (Laughter.)

Mr. Vicuña Mackenna having been loudly cheered, said that he thanked the gentlemen of the meeting for the profound and noble sympathy shown by them for his country, and himself personally ; that he did not propose to deliver an address, as he found himself unprepared for such an occasion, having come there only to hear the wonders of the telegraph ; that had he known he would have been called upon to speak, he would have been prepared to say something worthy of the attention of so many distinguished gentlemen. But as Mr. Collins, in his eloquent address, had mentioned his country several times with the applause of the assembly, he desired to be allowed to say that when

Secretary Seward addressed the governments of several nations in behalf of Mr. Collins' scheme, the government of his country was the first to answer the invitation, and offered its support to Mr. Collins, as Chili was fond of telegraphs, and of everything that meant progress. (Applause.) That they had more than one thousand miles of telegraph wire already laid out in the country before the war with Spain commenced; but that as soon as war was declared by Admiral Parejá, the Chilians replied to his dastardly attack somewhat as Columbus did to the Inquisition of Salamanca when they wanted to prevent his coming to discover this continent—ordering one thousand miles more of telegraph wire to be run for the internal defense of the country. (Applause.)

He further remarked that Chili, south of Panamá, was the only country in South America fitted for the Collins telegraph passing from the Pacific to the Atlantic, over the Pampas of Buenos Ayres; that this part of the line could be easily made in three or four months, as it was only one third of the length of the overland line to California, constructed, through the perseverance of Mr. Collins, in five months; that already the building of two railways was contemplated, to cross the Pampas from Chili to La Plata—the northern line from Copiapó to Rosario, on the Paraná River, and the other from Curicó south to Buenos Ayres; that two enterprising Americans were the promoters of these grand projects—the well-known Mr. Wheelwright, of Newburyport, of the northern line, and Henry Meiggs, of California, of the southern line. General Mitre, the enlightened and patriotic president of the Argentine Republic, a man who will stand forth prominently among the patriots of South America, had offered his warmest support to Mr. Meiggs' idea, believing that the best frontier against the wild Indian of the Pampas would be an iron track, which would thus spare the Argentine Republic the expense and the danger of maintaining six thousand soldiers to protect that part of the country from the raids of the savages. The orator added that another engineer, an American, too—Mr. Goldsborough—had laid before the Chilian Government a plan to build a submarine telegraph from Panamá to Valparaiso, running from port to port, on the line of the English steamers of the South Pacific.

Apropos of English commerce and enterprise in the South Pacific, Mr. Vicuña Mackenna observed, that not a single mercantile steam vessel, carrying the American flag, had been seen south of Panamá for years, and that through the fault of the Americans, that splendid field of commerce had been monopolized by the English since 1842, who maintained there a fine fleet of twenty or thirty steamers. He further observed that the Chilians would be grateful to England for having come to their relief in the war with Spain; because, although Mr. Blunt, in rather a blunt manner (laughter), remarked that England was prompted in that case by her copper interest, still, no matter why, she was sustaining their rights, and they would feel grateful to any country for coming forward from the same motive.

The speaker further observed that, although Chili was a great copper country, the Chilians were not *copperheads.* (Applause and laughter.) He advised the Americans to study the South American countries, especially Chili, to change their false policy towards them, and to go and see what they are. "Don't argue," he said, "that our doors are shut now, because if you go you will find some fair hand to open them. And then, gentlemen, if they are still shut, since you built the "Monnadnock" and the "Dunderberg," you have in your hands the keys of the world." (Applause.)

As in the course of his address, Mr.Collins, in a very pictorial manner, said that he purposed to enclose South America with a kind of North American *lasso,* in the form of a circular telegraph, Mr. Vicuña Mackenna closed his remarks with.the following words, which were enthusiastically received by the assembly :—I hope the day will come soon when the *lasso* of progress will enclose all the South American Republics, each one coming forward in support of Mr. Collins' enterprise. But allow me to remind you, gentlemen, that there is a yet more glorious and ancient *lasso* which binds the two continents of America in a single world of liberty and democracy; and that South American and North American *lasso* is the *Monroe Doctrine.*— (Great applause.)

Allow me further to say, that in South America we understand the Monroe Doctrine to be, not an empty word— not a platform word—not a newspaper word—we understand it as two great men of this country understand it—

as General Schenck understands it in Congress, and as
General Grant understands it on the field of battle : I
mean to say that we understand it at *the mouth of the
cannon.* (Renewed and great applause.)

A vote of thanks.was unanimously passed to the speaker;
and further, that his address should be printed at the expense of the Club. The meeting then adjourned.

The *New York Tribune,* of December 15th, gives the
following account of the proceedings of that session of the
New York Union League Club :

"Last evening, the regular monthly meeting of the
Union League Club was held at their rooms in East Seven-
teenth Street, Charles Butler, Esq., presiding.

After the transaction of business, Mr. P. McD. Collins
was introduced, and delivered the same lecture which he
read before the Travelers' Club on the 8th of November.

Señor Don Benjamin Vicuña Mackenna, Special Envoy
from Chili, was then introduced, who spoke as follows :

GENTLEMEN—After hearing such an eloquent lecture,
on a subject so interesting to the world, and by a man so
superior in intelligence, I think I am justified in saying
that your kindness in calling on me to speak amounts
almost to cruelty.

But as Mr. Collins has mentioned in his lecture the
name of my country, and I find myself among gentlemen
whom I consider friends of Chili, I venture to say that that
country was the first in South America to offer its cordial
and effective support to the great idea of encircling the
world with the telegraph. While, in fact, by its geographical position, Chili is in want of such a means of short-
ening distances, the telegraph will benefit it more than any
other nation, owing to its exclusion by nature from intercourse with other nations. Chili is fond of telegraphs—is
fond of everything that brings progress. (Applause.) We
had our pivot line of telegraphs in 1850, and now we have
the whole country spanned by them.

A line has been proposed from Panamá to Valparaiso.
Chili is the only country through which telegraph lines
could go from the Pacific to the Atlantic Ocean.—
It will not be adventurous to say that this line will soon
be completed.

I hope these facts will induce some of your enterprising
men to study it, and invest their capital.

Señor Mackenna alluded to the monopolizing of the commerce of Chili by England, a fact which he hoped would not long continue.

The speaker ended with a brilliant allusion to the Monroe doctrine. Its vital principle was the power which bound together the republics of this continent, and without which they could not exist. He hoped the time would come when it would be enunciated not only by editors and orators, but by such men as General Grant and General Schenck through the mouth of the cannon. (Immense applause.)

A vote of thanks to Señor Mackenna was passed unanimously."

ABRAHAM LINCOLN.

To the Hon. Thomas H. Nelson, Minister Plenipotentiary and Envoy Extraordinary from the United States of America to Chili, as a slight testimony of sincere friendship and profound sympathy with him in his just sorrow for the irreparable loss suffered by America in the death of ABRAHAM LINCOLN, sixteenth President of the United States.

> " One mournful wail is heard from shore to shore,
> *A Nation's* heart is stricken to the core ;
> And *Freedom,* kneeling with uncovered head,
> Weeps by the altar of *Our Country's Dead.*"
>
> ALBERT EVANS.—*On the Death of President Lincoln.*

I.

A sudden and overwhelming calamity has befallen America !

The bells of all the cities have tolled mournfully; the flags of all nations have been draped with the habiliments of woe ; all countenances display deep anguish; days of humiliation, fasting and prayer have been observed by all creeds—in a word, it may be said, without hyperbole, that the world discovered by Columbus has been overwhelmed with grief.

And wherefore ?

Is it perchance that tidings of some unheard-of catastrophe have been received at the same time throughout all countries ? Of fire, shipwreck, pestilence, overwhelming inundations ? What fearful plague has the wrath of Heaven let loose upon the earth ? Alas ! it is none of

these which make men's hearts grow faint and their fore-
heads bow low beneath the chastening rod! The horror of all that is about us has effaced from our minds
horror itself. And therefore it is that the most sanguinary battles fail to agonize the soul, that the martyrdom of
a people in one grand conflagration does not receive the
poor tribute of a memorial stone, and that the sudden
disappearance of a city reduced to atoms causes neither
dread nor wonder. Man of the present day, placed in the
vast camp of ruins called life, seems more wonder-stricken
at his own existence than at the unceasing destruction of
all created things, as he sees opening before his feet, ever
brilliant, ever fleeting, like the *ignis fatuus*, that other
chimera, the smiling mask of death—styled *futurity*.

What, then, has occurred?

Alas! That which has caused this deep, instanta-
neous, irrepressible sorrow in the hearts of all men—that
which has made the old man, the child and the maiden
alike leave their dwellings in search of the sad tiding—
that which has clothed all cities in mourning, and trans-
formed the whole of America, moved by one common sentiment, into one single altar for public prayer, into one
sepulchre—is the death of an HONEST MAN!

II.

Yes; Abraham Lincoln was not one of those great and
terrible beings known in history as Cæsar and Hannibal,
Charlemagne and Napoleon. His shoulders knew no
robes more regal than the simple dress of a citizen; no
crown encircled his forehead, save the sweat of rude and
honest toil; his arm wielded no other weapon than the
axe which felled the forest trees, that the ground they
shaded might yield the sweet fruits of the earth. He was,
on the contrary, that almost unknown being, an humble
apostle who had emerged from the forests of the Great
West to sit in the Capitol of the Rome of free ages, and
standing on the topmost of its steps, as it were on the
Sinai of Holy Writ, spoke to a multitude of down-trod-
den beings grovelling in the vilest servitude, or weighed
down by the chains placed upon them by the strong, and
said to them: " Be men! for there is but one humanity.
Be Christians! for there is but one God."

III.

There are men who have no ancestry and need them not. The world is their country—the human race their family. Abraham Lincoln was one of that class. No one knows with certainty from whence he came. All eyes are turned to the bright place whither he is going. His baptismal certificate would appear to be inscribed in the vault of that heaven whose brilliant rays illuminate his redeeming march; and, therefore, as he falls on one side the victim of an assassin's stroke, he is seen to rise, crowned with resplendent lights, to ascend to the highest place in the Kingdom of the Just!

The earthly life of such grand spirits is not an existence: it is a mission. Hence it is, that they make their appearance but at the interval of centuries. Between the initiatory mission of George Washington and the culminating mission of Abraham Lincoln, the American race had passed through an entire era.

The *colonist* and the *slave* were the two extremes of that grand spiritual transformation of the inhabited globe known as "Democracy."

Washington changed the first into a *citizen*, and passed away, great, sublime, almost sanctified, to be claimed by all ages.

Lincoln changed the second into a *man*, and for this he falls a martyr; the whole earth his sepulchre.

Heroes in goodness ! Blessed be ye throughout all ages and amongst all men !

IV.

But who was Abraham Lincoln, as a moral being and as a character, as the living agent of that supreme goodness which seemed to be incorporated with, and a very part of, his immortal spirit ? That is what we shall endeavor to show in these hastily prepared lines. Some incidents, made known by sorrowing and absent friends, and a few of those pages, covered with the emblems of mourning, which have been scattered by the press, are all that we have with which to delineate to our countrymen that noble figure of goodness, which should be attempted only by the greatest artists, and not by our feeble hand.

V.

Abraham Lincoln was born in the midst of the primeval forests of America, on the banks of the Ohio, and not far from the Mississippi, the first the finest, and the other the largest of North American rivers. His father was a laborer; his grandfather was a colonist-soldier, and perished at his own door, while defending his home from the savages. In the midst of those Kentucky woods, on the 12th of February, 1809, came into the world, he whose name, for ages to come, shall never be uttered save with the veneration inspired by the great Redeemer's, with the love felt for all public benefactors, and with the sorrow due to all sublime martyrs.

"Abraham Lincoln (said one of the journals opposed to him, as in mockery of his humble origin), this honest old lawyer, with face half Roman, half Indian, passed his first years in the western wilds, grappling with remonstrating bears, and looking out for the too frequent rattlesnake. Tall, strong, lithe and smiling, Abe toiled on as farm-laborer, mule-driver, sheep-feeder, deer-killer, wood-cutter, and, lastly, as boatman on the waters of the Wabash and the Mississippi."

VI.

Such was the childhood and youth of Abraham Lincoln. When but seven years of age, in 1816, he left the Kentucky forests on the southern bank of the Ohio, for those on the other side of the river in the State of Indiana. Fourteen years later, in 1830, he again moved from the Indiana forests into the still more savage ones of Illinois, on the confines of the region then inhabited by the savages whose arrow's had, years before, caused the death of his grandsire. These two trips, or rather this progressive march of the Western settler, which marked two epochs in the obscure life of Abraham Lincoln, had presented but one contrast, but one simple and natural change—which was, that in the first he was carried by his father with the rest of his family, in a wagon drawn by oxen, whilst in the latter, it was he who, being more fit for work, guided the vehicle which carried his household goods to the Far West.

7

On his arrival in Illinois, the young settler found himself—as had his grandfather—with gun in hand, to resist the invasion of the aboriginal tribes. In the war with the Indians, known as the Black Hawk War, he was elected by his companions Captain of Volunteers.

VII.

During all this time, Abraham Lincoln had been to school but for six months. But there are beings who derive their learning from all that they see, or that they hear, or that comes into their hands, whether printed or written—books, newspapers, paintings, objects of nature, —in a word, all that can be acquired from books, as ideas or as syntheses ; and Abraham Lincoln's was one of those deep minds which gather, from observation and comparison, an immense store of intellectual wealth and practical knowledge.

By said means, Abraham Lincoln became a lawyer in 1835.

He was not a lawyer graduated at a University ; he had no diploma, and could scarcely count twenty-seven years of a poor and uneventful life ; but the moral power which was raising him to the glorious end in store for him, soon placed him at the summit of the profession which he had selected.

In 1845, Abraham Lincoln was the best lawyer in the State of Illinois.

VIII.

But Abraham Lincoln was not like all other lawyers. Having had no masters, neither had he colleagues, nor numerous but haughty clients, such as gather round the jurists in vogue. For him, the Forum was not an arena for ambition, nor a field camp in which to strive for scholastic renown; it was not even the tribunal of science, and much less the place for acquiring wealth. It was something nobler, for he was more humble and disinterested. For that athlete of the forests, the Forum was the tribunal of God's justice; it was the throne of the law, sublime goddess of that modern paganism, stigmatized by Rome, called *Human Democracy*, simple formula of the Old Gospel which proclaimed the equality of men; it was, in fine, the portico of charity where the unfortunate sought refuge from the strong, and where all persecuted virtue found a shelter.

That was the diadem of Abraham Lincoln—the starting-point in his grand mission of humanity. Mercy, tenderness, love for the good, respect for man, pity for the afflicted, and, above all, his perfect,unquestioned and sublime honesty. Abraham Lincoln was the advocate of the poor, of all the widows and orphans of Illinois; and therefore lived in an humble way, with no other happiness and no other pride than his wife and children, his sole income being his daily bread, blessed by the lips of thousands.

In that simple home, the sole inheritance of the martyr's children, lived, for twenty-five years, the very personification of unspotted honor, that " Honest Abe," whom the American people mourn as for a father, and bless almost as a saint. It was there in his old homestead, in Springfield, that his fellow-countrymen sought him to carry him to that Capitol in Washington, from the summit of which it seems as though the whole world might be surveyed; and there he now rests in the eternal sleep of this earthly nothingness, after having received, in his passage from the Presidential Chair to the tomb—not the angry oath of those who shook the bloody tunic of Caesar in the Forum, crying for vengeance!—but the grandest Apotheosis within the memory of ages, as a tribute from a free people to a citizen.

IX.

As a political man, Abraham Lincoln had but one principle—Liberty, as, when a lawyer, he had but one aim—Justice. Therefore, before being called to the Presidential Chair of Washington's successors, had his voice for truth and liberty already been heard at public meetings, and in the halls of Congress on two solemn occasions in the history of the American nation. The first was when the accursed ambition of the men of the South carried into Mexico the banner of the Stars, veiled with the crape of the usurpers. Abraham Lincoln, placing himself by the side of the noble Clay, and from the seat which he occupied by the votes of his fellow-citizens, as a representative in Congress from Illinois, denounced before the world the crime of that oligarchy of slavery, which wished to usurp the territories lying south of the Union, to plant therein the seed of slavery, accursed of God and condemned by the human law of all times.

The second proof was in 1858, when those same men attempted to gain, through political trickery, the territories of the North, in order to introduce into that virgin soil their black institutions, by repealing the so-called " Missouri Compromise," which had, since 1820, prevented the propagation of slavery into the North by a barrier as of granite, for it was the barrier of the law.

Abraham Lincoln had then become the hope of a party. The Republicans were organizing in those days of preparation, under the rallying cry of " No more slavery in free territories." The Democrats, who were already meditating the bloody catastrophe, which has been termed the " Rebellion," put forward, on their side, as opponent to the rising athlete of the West, in this conflict, or rather in this skirmish preliminary to the grand struggle, the man of the South whom they considered their champion, the famous Stephen Douglass, known as the *little giant* on account of his small stature and colossal eloquence. They were both candidates for seats in the United States Senate from the State of Illinois. They contested face to face, day by day, and hour by hour, by speech, by argument, and at the ballot-box. The popular voice was in favor of Abraham Lincoln, but the votes of the State Legislature elected his rival, and Abraham Lincoln yielded a willing submission, for the choice was made in accordance with the law.

X.

But his defeat was his most glorious victory. He had entered the lists as a soldier in a just cause, and though defeated now, he was to rise again as leader in that cause. Few men—says a California journalist, as he draws, with masterly hand, the necrology of President Lincoln, referring to the above-mentioned electioneering canvass of 1858,—were able to cope with Stephen Douglass ; but Abraham Lincoln was. In the force and logic of his arguments, in the style of eloquence requisite to move the masses of the West, in his readiness with answers, in his just criteria, iu the art of captivating and convincing vast assemblages, he had but few superiors.

Even that great and discontented distributor of all high reputations—the *London Times*—said, when giving an account of a book which was published, with the debates upon slavery, between Douglass and Lincoln, in Illinois, that this "obscure Western lawyer" had by himself thrown more novelty and light upon that old subject, than was due to Wilberforce and Lord Brougham, the great English abolitionists, to the most illustrious opponents of slavery in the American Union—Henry Clay and Daniel Webster.

The reputation of Abraham Lincoln was already made, for it had crossed the Atlantic.

XI.

Be it as it might, Lincoln, though defeated by Douglass in Illinois, in 1858, in his turn triumphed over the latter in all the free States in 1860; and Abraham Lincoln, the "rail-splitter" of Hardin County, Kentucky, and the plain lawyer of Springfield, was inaugurated President of the United States on the 4th of March, 1861.

The farewell words of Lincoln on that occasion to the town of his love were, like his own soul, pure and full of tenderness.

"My friends," said he, betraying much emotion, as he addressed the inhabitants of Springfield for the last time, on the 11th of February, 1861—"my friends, no one not in my position can appreciate the sadness I feel at this parting. To this people I owe all that I am. Here I have lived more than a quarter of a century; here my children were born; and here one of them lies buried. I know not how soon I shall see you again. A duty devolves upon me which is, perhaps, greater than that which has devolved upon any other man since the days of Washington. He never could have succeeded except for the aid of Divine Providence, upon which he at all times relied. I feel that I cannot succeed without the same Divine aid which sustained him; and in the same Almighty Being I place my reliance for support; and I hope you, my friends, will all pray that I may receive that Divine assistance, without which I cannot succeed, but with which success is certain. Again, I bid you all an affectionate farewell."

The man who had secured all the votes of Illinois, now carried away with him all their hearts.

XII.

Not less noble nor ingenuous was his inaugural address on the 4th of March, 1861, delivered in the presence of the American Congress, the majority of which was opposed to him politically. He spoke to the legislators of his country as he had spoken to the obscure voters of Springfield—with a heart overflowing with goodness, love, and hope of reconciliation and happiness.

"My countrymen," he cried, as he closed that famous address, and after protesting that he should never attempt to interfere with the sovereign right of any slave State in the Union to manage their own institutions—"My countrymen, one and all, think calmly and well upon this whole subject. Nothing valuable can be lost by taking time.

"If there be an object to hurry any of you in hot haste to a step which you would never take deliberately, that object will be frustrated by taking time; but no good object can be frustrated by it.

"Such of you as are now dissatisfied still have the old Constitution unimpaired, and on the sensitive point the laws of your own framing under it; while the new administration will have no immediate power, if it would, to change either.

"If it were admitted that you who are dissatisfied hold the right side in the dispute, there is still no reason for precipitate action. Intelligence, patriotism, Christianity, and a firm reliance on Him who has never yet forsaken this favored land, are still competent to adjust, in the best way, all our present difficulties.

"In your hands, my dissatisfied fellow-countrymen, and not in mine, is the momentous issue of civil war. The Government will not assail you.

"You can have no conflict without being yourselves the aggressors. You have no oath registered in Heaven to destroy the Government; while I shall have the most solemn one to preserve, protect, and defend it.

"I am loath to close. We are not enemies, but friends. We must not be enemies. Though passion may have strained, it must not break our bonds of affection.

"The mystic cords of memory, stretching from every battle field and patriot grave to every living heart and hearth-stone all over this broad land, will yet swell the chorus of the Union, when again touched, as surely they will be, by the better angels of our nature."

What other man ever used like language to his fellow-citizens, to his enemies, to the avowed conspirators against his authority ? In vain would we look for two passages in any way approaching those just quoted, in those meaningless array of words, commonly called *Messages*, of the sovereigns to their people.

XIII.

The doings, the sufferings, the purposes of Abraham Lincoln during the four years of his first tumultuous presidential term, and up to the moment when the parricidal bullet pierced through the walls of his mighty intellect, all are known to the whole world, and his glory would gain nothing by a single additional note, obscure and unknown, to the infinite hymn now being sung in his honor by all freemen throughout the universe. But here we wish to recall to the memory of all another noble act.— When McClellan, in 1862, was forced to abandon the first siege of Richmond, the people of Washington, exasperated at the disaster, held a war meeting to denounce the Secretary of War, at whose door the blame of the failure was laid. The excitement was intense; but lo! in the midst of the multitude appears one who is greeted with vociferous applause by all. It was the President of the United States! Without the least hesitation, he ascends the stand prepared for the public speakers, and, after a short address, he utters words, worthy to be eternally remembered.

"We know nothing greater in the political history of mankind than that trait of noble patriotism, manly loyalty, and truly sublime and christian humility, unless it be that other eminently American act of the transfer which took place at Washington of the supreme power when Abraham Lincoln breathed his last. The transfer of the most extensive civil and military power, whether on land or at sea, of the present day, was made with the same simplicity with which the patriarchs of old used to divide

the inheritance of their tribe amongst their offspring.—
That Napoleon I, might receive the crown upon his tem-
ples beneath the banners of Notre Dame at Paris, it was
necessary for him to deluge Europe in blood for ten long
years. That Andrew Johnson might be invested with the
supreme rule of 'the most powerful nation of modern
times, nothing more was requisite than a simple message
to a hotel, and a conversation rather thon a ceremony of a
few moments duration in a private room.

XIV.

The rigid loyalty of Abraham Lincoln·in the presence of
public assemblages never swerved before any power, never
gave way to any passion. Abraham Lincoln, calm and
alert as a skilful pilot in a storm, always used the same
language to the loyal people and to the people in rebellion;
to the Congress of the United States asking for information, and to the public gatherings who called him to his
balconies seeking his aid or counsel; to the powerful Government of Great Britain, to whom he returned Slidell
and Mason in the name of the law, and to weaker Brazil,
whose flag he caused to be saluted, as homage due to justice violated by force.

XV.

In this respect, Abraham Lincoln was one of the most
uncommon and greatest of men, because, as a political
man, he possessed the love of truth—that grand and rare
virtue amongst the politicians who now rule the world.—
He was the founder of a new school. He took upon himself to prove to the world that the conscience of an honest
man was better for governing a nation than all the cannons of brute force, and all the intrigues of cunning and
perfidy. Prior to his appearance, to govern was to lie.—
Now, falsehood, like a fetid torch, would be extinguished
on the white marble of his tomb. Before him, Franklin
Pierce had, by that human abomination which courtiers
loudly applaud, and style "intriguing ability," placed the
Union on the brink of the abyss into which it was afterwards precipitated by James Buchanan's decrepit imbe-
cility—convenient pabulum of the felony of thousands of
hidden traitors for four long years. But Lincoln raised

from the ground his criminally betrayed country, restored her to her ancient glory, placed in her hand the sword of justice, and on her forehead the brilliant diadem of truth.

Abraham Lincoln, as chief ruler of one of the great powers of modern times, reduced all books on diplomacy to one single principle—good faith; interpreted all international codes in one way—justice; and brushed away all the schemes and artifices of politicians with one single tool—the truth.

XVI.

Abraham Lincoln was never guilty of falsehood. All that he ever did was pre-announced by himself as to the time and manner in which he would do; and when the hour fixed arrived, his promise was fulfilled though the whole world might interpose. In his inaugural message, for example, he said that he wished not to interfere with the question of slavery in the Southern States, in order to give them no pretext for rebellion; and although the pressure of his party bore heavily upon his will and action to induce him to revoke that promise, he would never do so, neither in the moments of exultation because of glorious victories, nor in the midst of panics because of disasters.

A little later, in a proclamation which shall henceforth be placed in the annals of America by the side of Washington's farewell address, he announced that slavery would be declared abolished in all rebel States which should not have submitted on a fixed day and hour, and on that day and hour four millions of human beings were made free.

XVII.

Thus were laid for all times the foundations of a policy totally at variance with the old course of the world. The policy or doctrine of Monroe was an energetic but egotistical expansion of American strength within its own orbit. Lincoln's policy was the extension of universal conscience throughout all ends of the earth. The doctrine of the first was a menace to Europe. The policy of the latter is a lesson to the world; and, now that that doctrine has been consecrated by the blood of its author, all ages shall take upon themselves to convert the belief of the *just* into the religion of all who love *justice*.

XVIII.

We have said all that we know of Abraham Lincoln.—
Such was he as a lawyer, statesman, and chief magistrate.
We will now look at him as a man.

The noblest virtues which adorned that grand figure of
modern times, were the loving kindness of his character,
and the magnanimous clemency of his soul.

Never, during those four years of frightful struggle, in
which blood poured as from a heaven darkened by the
most horrible passions, and the smoke of gigantic battles,
never was that humble but most powerful man heard to
utter an angry, not even a bitter word against his enemies and those of his country.   His favorite saying was
one of the noblest sentences of Christianity—" Forgive
them, Lord, for they know not what they do."   That was
the emblem of the hate with which his heart returned the
hatred of his adversaries; that was the sole reply of Liberty's high priest to the thousand foul tongues which day
by day poured the venom of calumny upon his noble head;
that was, perchance, the sublime meditation of that spirit
of mercy so clearly pictured in his long suffering face, at
the very moment when the parricide's stroke chilled on his
lips his last habitual smile.   And that was, we cannot
doubt; his last and only vengeance, as, in his tranquil and
silent agony, raising his thoughts to that God whom he
ever invoked, he prayed, in humble imitation of the
spotless Lamb of Calvary, for the pardon of his slayers.
Alas ! why do men like Abraham Lincoln die, when so
many cruel tyrants, so many vile doers of crime, so many
oppressors of humanity, robed in the purple of the Cæsars,
or in the worn-out mantle of the sellers in the Temple,
still live in all their pomp and sin ?   Why did not the
guardian angel of America, that tutelary genius who
closed in peace the eyes of Freedom's greatest heroes—
Washington and Bolivar, San Martin and Franklin—why
did he not stay the slayer's arm, as in the case mentioned
in Holy Writ, and which is brought to our mind by the
name of our great martyr, and once more fulfil that law
of salvation which has redeemed from danger so many
precious lives ?

God alone knows !

Meanwhile, the sentence of destiny had gone forth;

and therefore was consummated the greatest crime the
world ever saw, in audacity, combination, and success; in
the choice of place, hour, and occasion; in the motives
alleged; in all its episodes and parties; in a word, that
tragedy of a second's duration, in which appeared the
horrible and terrible spectre, Wilkes Booth, the most atro-
cious and the most daring of all criminals who have be-
queathed their names to history. Truly, in order to sacrifice in such a manner so kind, so merciful a man, one
so full of all goodness as Abraham Lincoln, it needed that
in the universe there should also dwell a man with heart
devoured by the flames of hell, and whose assassin arm
should be strengthened with the terrible energy of the
reprobate.

To slay Nero, the arm of a cowardly and base slave
sufficed. Cain alone could have murdered Abel!

XIX.

In the honors which have been rendered to the great
martyr of the age, in the tears which have been shed, and
in the eulogiums which have been made by all mankind,
there has been nothing fictitious or conventional. The
liberation of the slaves had inscribed his name on the
golden page of the saviours of humanity, which commenced with Moses, and had been closed with Washington.

His unbounded toleration of all creeds, all systems, and
all things not condemned by law and justice, those eternal
attributes of all nations, had made him the citizen of all
countries, and therefore all have mourned for him as for a
personal loss. His very enemies have furnished the noblest
and most expressive epitaphs for his tomb. General Lee,
on hearing of the crime, exclaimed, as his eyes filled with
tears, "The man has gone who conquered the South before and more effectually than all the armies of Grant!"
and that other remark of the implacable rebel, General
Roger Pryor—"The best friend of the South has gone,"
are not they of themselves the brightest crown of all which,
in his funeral apotheosis, decked the brow cold in death
of the dictator of good ?

XX.

In his private habits, Abraham Lincoln was worthy of

the ancient name he bore. He lived as did the patriarchs
of the early ages, with no other pleasures than love for
his kin; with no other goods than the roof under which
he passed his days; no other worship than that of God.—
He belonged to no sect; he recognized the mystic supre-
macy of no church; but he was, notwithstanding, the
most fervent christian, the most generous philanthropist,
the sincerest and humblest of believers, as is shown by his
speeches, harangues, messages to Congress, and, in short,
by everything which fell from his lips or was written by
his pen, which were ever clothed in the vastest and truest
religious spirit. His enemies said that he only wrote *ser-
mons*, because they could not understand that he, the gen-
eralissimo on sea and land, who commanded the largest
armies and most formidable squadrons of which history
speaks, was but a simple priest of Liberty; a humble and
sublime liberator, who had come from the forests of the
West to rule half a world with the two codes which contained all his belief and all his duties—the Constitution
of the Union and the Holy Bible.

XXI.

But from all that has been said, it may, perchance, be
thought that Abraham Lincoln was a grave, pertinacious,
inflexible man. And, nevertheless, there was not in the
United States a plainer, more jovial, and humorous man.
The merry and jocose humor of "Old Abe" was prover-
bial, not only in the servants' rooms in the White House
at Washington, but also in the cabins of the most
unhappy slaves. He was ever laughing, ever joyous, and
always accessible. A joke was the chief characteristic of
his conversations in the family circle, as a certain biblical
tone pervaded all that he said or wrote concerning his
public mission. He could not converse without relating
an anecdote, nor write without quoting from some
parable.

On one occasion, while traveling in a stage coach, in
1848, making the circuit of the Illinois courts, he pre-
tended to be an ignorant countryman, and made a young
lawyer, his fellow-passenger, relate the most absurd stories about the comet which appeared that year. But his
credulity, which he kept up to the end, was but an inno-

cent joke, perfectly proper on such an occasion. On the following day, he saluted his astounded colleague as Abraham Lincoln, the Nestor of the Illinois Bar. Fifteen years later, on delivering to the aforesaid young lawyer his credentials as Minister to one of the American Republics, he recalled to his memory the story of the comet with that ingenuous mirth which is the frankincense of all good souls.

It is also told of him, that when our Envoy, Rear-Admiral Simpson, was presented to him, for the purpose of obtaining the permission of his Government to build ships of war for Chile in the ship yard of the United States, he gave the refusal in a peculiar characteristic manner. "We will receive you," said he, "as Envoy of a nation which we highly esteem, as a librarian receives all who visit his rooms. You shall have all at your disposal, look at everything, examine everything ; but then you cannot have a single thing ; you may not carry away the book lent to you, for it is my duty to return it safely to its place."

XXII.

Abraham Lincoln joined, to a sound, practical judgment, common to men of his race, the most exquisite simplicity of language. It was said of him that no man in the United States could say more in fewer words, nor greater things in more humble language. The frugality of his habits could be compared only with the modesty of his character. Never did he drink any kind of liquor during his long and austere life, nor did he even allow himself the innocent use of tobacco. His dress was as unpretending as that of the old Puritans. In Washington, as at Springfield, he used to buy the first suit he saw in a tailor's show-window; and had his wardrobe been appraised at the time of his death, it would not have been valued at more than that of his predecessor and friend, General Taylor, who, while President of the United States, was wont to appear in the streets of Washington in a common suit, the total value of which was estimated by passers-by at "nine dollars."

XXIII.

His personal looks did not fail to harmonize with his

disregard for appearances. That man, gifted as he was, with such rich qualities of soul and mind, had, like the opaque vase of Scripture, a common, almost vulgar, look. He was very tall, bony, thin and gaunt, and his coarse features gave no signs of the gentleness of his soul, save in that ever present smile which death itself found playing round his lips. He was the backwoodsman of the West, removed to the Capitol at Washington, in all his original rusticity, which seemed to lend increased strength to his innate power. He was the same wood-cutter of the Ohio, seated on the throne of human democracy, save that the destinies of the world now depended upon his axe !

XXIV.

Such was Abraham Lincoln, the liberator of the slaves —the new Moses who dictated to the disinherited race of Ham the tables of the covenant like unto those received on Sinai by the Hebrew people—the people of the Saviour of mankind—Jesus Christ.

He lived an honest man, and died, like the saints of the Christian calendar, anointed with blood and the glory of martyrdom. His grand mission of humanity, of duty, and responsibility, being ended, he had not, like Washington at Mount Vernon, or Jackson at the Hermitage, that last happiness of great and toil-worn men, a peaceful death at the close of the long and arduous work to which they were called on earth by the Supreme Distributor of callings.

Neither did he close his eyes in death, as did his predecessors, Adams, Jefferson, and Monroe, on the great day of their country, as though that country wished to display its brightest gems as she gathered them for ever into her bosom. °   °   °   ° Abraham Lincoln ceased to exist on a still more solemn day. The redeemer of the slaves died on the day on which the Redeemer of all mankind was crucified on Calvary !

Let his memory be blessed throughout all ages to come !

XXV.

And until those ages shall arrive, with their royal offerings of reward and justice, let thy name, oh ! Abraham Lincoln ! be known and proclaimed as Benefactor by all

the oppressed of the earth; let thy memory be glorified with
hymns of gratitude and praise by all free men who know
thy origin, wood-cutter of the forest, and have heard of
thy end, oh ! martyr of liberty ! Let thy new redeeming
doctrine of government, clothed in the white robe of that
grand truth, unspotted as it came from thee, be inscribed
in the book of the destinies of the New World, by the side
of Washington's *Farewell* and Monroe's *Doctrine*—those
two covenants of that American democracy of the propagation of which they were the first apostles, as thou hast
just been made the martyr. Let thy simple homestead at
Springfield be consecrated by the ovations of the world
as the humble temple of thy humble virtues; let thy love
for all that was good, and for thy fellow-men, let thy
veneration for home and family, let thy constant fear of
the All-Powerful and of thy country's verdict, sole guide
of thy guiltless conscience—let thy charity for all who,
hungry in body or soul, thou feddest with thy bread or
didst relieve with thy wisdom—let all these, like a choir
of angels, be grouped around thy tomb, with all the
other emblems of those sublime gifts which have made thy
name conspicuous amongst those of thy fellow-beings—
thy Probity and thy Poverty !

Yes ! oh, Abraham Lincoln ! blessed be thy poverty,
at which the proud and haughty ones did scoff, whom thou
didst afterwards humble and subdue but to pardon ; and
which covers with shame and confusion all those who,
born like thyself, did not know how to remain poor when
powerful as thou wast, humble dictator of a world of
opulency !

Yes ! oh, Abraham Lincoln ! let thy grave, opened by
the tears of thy fellow-countrymen, in the very centre of
thy glorious Union, serve henceforth, as Washington's at
Mount Vernon, for an altar of consolation and oblations
to the pilgrim who searches throughout the universe for
the worship of his persecuted creed; to the exile who bears
on his forehead the impress of cruel tyranny; to the emigrant who comes to thy soil in search of bread for his
loved ones; to the negro-slave who shall journey from all
lands and from all islands wherever thy voice may have
broken his fetters, to ask for his tutelary genius and to
bless him; to the human race, in fine, who acknowledges
thee as an apostle of truth, as a creator of a new era in

the reign of ideas, as the greatest reformer of the political principles which have ruled or misguided peoples and governments, and as the purest and most innocent martyr, the one most capable of every heroism and every virtue who ever fell beneath the hand of a parricide !

And for all this, oh, Abraham Lincoln ! on this soil of distant Chili, on which are raised monuments to the martyrs of ideas and victims of the fanatical, let there b one offering worthy of thy glorification after thy martyrdom; for thou too didst love our land and serve it; for with the breath of thy spotless integrity thou didst efface for ever from the altar of our alliance that reproach of idolatry of money which the greediness of covetous traders had ever shown for its never filled coffer; because thou didst repay the joy with which we heard of thy victories with the ingenuous thanks so often expressed in thy despatches, ever brilliant with the sincerity of thy language; because thou alone, of all the powerful, didst remember that on certain grand but ignored days, there was, on the soil of thy country, a tri-colored flag, the banner of our nation, and didst order honors to be paid to it not rendered to the standards of the powerful; and because, noble and good friend of Chile, as thou didst look around over the diaphanic firmament of nature, thou didst more than once contemplate, with loving look, that lone star, the symbol of our destiny, twin-sister of those on thy once again intact banner, and which, like them, shall shine until time shall be no more, with the resplendent brilliancy of fixed stars, never with the borrowed light of satellites.

And for all this also, oh, Abraham Lincoln ! whilst Europe exhumes from the dust of ages the figures which embody its perverse idolatry of usurpers and tyrants, America, ever independent, ever free, ever democratic, will return the challenge of monarchies, by presenting to the eyes of the world thine immortal image and by venerating thy name, a thousand-fold greater than all the ancient Cæsars, again restored to life, as that of a common father who from high heaven unites, with loving hands, into one single family, at once respected and powerful, those two grand divisions of the earth and of the human race, known as the World of Columbus.

B. VICUÑA MACKENNA.

Santiago, June 1st, 1865.

MOTION

Offered in the House of Deputies of Chile, at their
Meeting of 3d June, 1865.

———

The name of ABRAHAM LINCOLN, sixteenth President
of the United States of North America, has been, for the
past four years, to all the nations of South America, and
especially to Chile, the most conspicuous and characteristic emblem of the Democratic institutions which
prevail in the greater part of the countries of the New
World.

By his most noble fulfilment of his difficult and great
mission, no less than by the exalted qualities of his character, had that eminent citizen attained, in the opinion
of the Chilian people, to the same height at which our
seniors, half a century since, contemplated the figure of
George Washington first President of the Union, and beyond doubt the true initiator of the independence of both
continents of America.

But to the bright gems of his high personal merits and
of his honest, just and freedom-giving policy, the tragic
and sudden death of President Lincoln, at the very moment in which he was about closing the great work of social reconstruction which he had undertaken, giving life
and civil liberty to four millions of human beings, has
added to his renown the glory of a noble martyrdom, at
the sight of which the heart of all true Americans has
been shrouded in mourning.

And of all the nations of our Continent and people of
our race, Chilians have especial reasons to offer their sympathy and sorrow to the people and Government of the
United States, for the irreparable loss of that man who
from all points of view was great.

From the time that Abraham Lincoln took in hand the helm of State, in 1861, his equitable and justice-loving policy commenced to clear away, with admirable zeal, all pending difficulties for many years previous between Chile and his country, thus giving us a true mark of consideration, which some of his predecessors denied us, and bringing about in this manner the most cordial relations of mutual esteem and friendship between the two countries.

In view of events within the memory of all, it may be said, unhesitatingly, that during the existence of Chile, as as an independent nation, she has had no more faithful or considerate friend than the United States Government, under President Lincoln's administration.

Since the date of the not only pacific but cordial and respectful settlement of the old Macedonian question, until the spontaneous offer of mediation, made in the name of the Government of the United States, by their most worthy representative in Chili, in our late difficulty with Bolivia, it may be said that the Chilian people and government have been the constant recipients of marks of sympathy and esteem from the American people and government.

It is pleasing to us now to remember that the first and most condoling diplomatic note addressed to the Government of this Republic, after the terrible calamity by which it was afflicted in December of 1863, was that of the Representative of the United States, at the same time that the Cabinet at Washington was, of its own volition, taking part with us in our national rejoicings, by issuing orders that simple, though significant, honors should be paid to our flag and Representative on the national holidays of Chile, thus giving an unprecedented example of national courtesy towards us, and which will therefore always form a highly honorable exception to our Republic.

The sincere tokens of appreciation and reciprocal generosity which the Government of President Lincoln constantly evinced for our political course, reached to the point of giving liberty, on our last September anniversary, —and for no other reason than that he was a Chilian— to a criminal lying in prison under sentence of the Courts.

But, aside from all these considerations, so suitable to excite a vote of sincere friendship from the Representatives of the Chilian people, the fact alone of the termination of the war, and the reconstruction of the North American Union, gives such reassurances of actual safety and peaceful future to South American Republics, that for the conscientious discharge of our public duty, as well as in accordance with a true policy, it becomes us to offer to the American people our cordial congratulations upon the restoration of internal peace and the triumph of those democratic principles which have been so tenaciously, although secretly, fought against by European Governments, giving unseen aid to the Southern States in rebellion—those same Governments which, since the commencement of that rebellion, have been plotting and scheming against our safety and our honor.

And, again, the civil war in the United States was, of itself, so horrible a calamity, that its termination should receive from all Christian nations of the earth—and especially from the Chilian people, who had watched with such intensely heartfelt interest the terrible incidents of that struggle—an expression of profound gratitude to that Divine Providence who has so happily ended a scourge unequaled and unknown in the annals of nations and of time.

Thus it appears to have been understood by the Government of Chile, when, in the last message of the chief of the nation, the restoration of peace in the United States was spoken of as the most notable event of the present time, and expression was given to the nation's sorrow at the bloody sacrifice of the great man to whose laudable policy of good faith and honesty, more than to the triumph of his armies, was due that happy consummation.

The Government of the Republic has, therefore, duly fulfilled its duties. The people of Chile have done likewise, having given on this, as on all former occasions, those worthy and appropriate manifestations of their feelings which have gained so high a place for our name in the public opinion of foreign nations. It is, therefore, right that in its turn the Congress of Chile, as the true representative of the people, should likewise offer a simple tribute, but at the same time worthy and expressive of the sentiments which animate that body in presence of the two-fold character of the late intelligence from North America.

In view of these observations, of the justice of which I doubt not all the representatives of the Chilean nation will agree, I have not hesitated to submit to your votes an idea which, in my humble opinion, covers the different feelings which at this moment animate us, and which is expressed in the following

PROJECT OF LAW:

ARTICLE 1st—The portraits of George Washington and Abraham Lincoln, the first and last Presidents of the United States of America, shall be procured at the nation's cost, and placed in the Reception Hall of the Department of Foreign Affairs of Chile, as a tribute offered by the Chilean people to that of the United States, on the occasion of the restoration of their internal peace and their mournful loss in the death of their Chief Magistrate.

ARTICLE 2d—This *project of law* shall be appropriately inscribed at the foot of the aforesaid portraits, and communicated by the Government of Chile to the President of the Senate and Speaker of the House of Representatives of the United States, as an expression of the feelings of the Chilean Congress.

ARTICLE 3d—The President of the Republic is hereby authorized to carry this *project of law* into effect.

This authorization to be in force for the term of six months.

BENJAMIN VICUÑA MACKENNA.

SANTIAGO, June 3, 1865.

POSTSCRIPT.

Attempted Arrest of B. Vicuña Mackenna, Confidential Agent of Chili in
the United States, with the Preliminaries of his Trial for Alleged Viola-
tion of the Neutrality Laws of the latter country, " in fitting out an
¡ ! Armed Expedition against the Dominions of the Queen of Spain."

Although it was not our intention to devote any space
to the subject referred to above, we deem it interesting,
particularly to the readers of this pamphlet who
have given their attention to the proceedings and
opinions on the Monroe Doctrine, and the feeling exhibited on that occasion by the people of the United States, to
understand how those opinions and feelings have been carried out in reference to the so-called " sister republic " of
Chili by *the Government of the United States.*

We purposely refrain from any commentary. The facts
to which the following documents refer speak for themselves.

On the 6th of February, just a month after the great
Monroe Doctrine meeting took place, and on which
occasion the letter from the Hon. District Attorney,
Daniel S. Dickinson, expressing his warmest sympathies
with the cause of the republic against the attempts of the
European monarchies (see page 64), was read, Mr. Vicuña
Mackenna, confidential agent of the Republic of Chili,
now at war with the Spanish Monarchy, was arrested at
his residence by order of the above functionary, as appears from the following letter, addressed by Mr. Vicuña
Mackenna to the Editor of the *New York Herald*, on the
8th of February.

NEW YORK, Feb. 8, 1866.

The *New York Herald*, and most of the daily papers of this city, having published erroneous statements concerning the attempted arrest made of my person by the United States Marshal on the evening of the 6th inst, I hope that you will permit me to state the facts in the case, and place this affair, with which the public is so intensely interested, in its true light. What really took place is simply as follows :

I was enjoying the quiet of my residence when I was informed that one or several persons unknown to me wished to see me. As I have given the strictest orders to the servants to admit no one to my presence without first bringing me their names, their admission was denied. Nevertheless, my private secretary, who expressly occupies a room for the reception of those who solicit interviews with me, so as to leave me free from the innumerable importunates who assail my house every day, received the persons who sought me, and inquired the object of their visit, such being the instructions which he had received.

The United States Marshal, who came accompanied by five officers, resorted at the commencement to subterfuges altogether unnecessary; but as soon as he declared his name and business, my secretary ascended to my room, and I at once went down stairs to present myself to that functionary.

I asked to see the warrant of arrest, and, after having read it, quietly observed that I could not be arrested, because, although my position in this country had been that of special agent of Chili, I could also claim diplomatic immunity as Secretary of the Chilean Legation at Washington, which title I had in my possession, and could show then and there.

The Marshal, who conducted himself with the utmost courtesy and respect, as also his subordinates, went to consult the United States District Attorney, and I despatched several telegrams to Washington, so that the Chilian Minister might take the necessary steps with the Secretary of State.

After the lapse of half an hour the Marshal returned, and told me that I might remain in my house, go to the opera, or wherever I saw fit, and that one or two officers would accompany me with all due respect.

I accepted these conditions; and one deputy-marshal only having remained—Mr. Robinson, an extremely civil young man—he did me the honor to dine with me and accompany me to the house of my banker, the highly-respectable and worthy merchant, Mr. George G. Hobson; and to the house of my counsel, Mr. E. W. Stoughton, returning afterwards to his house, and I to mine, where I slept free of the custody of any one.

All the mysterious details, the novel incidents, and the inventions of all sorts published by the press, are each and all of them fictions, gotten up to excite curiosity, or have, perhaps, been dictated by less noble motives. I have been assured that Spanish agents were found in the neighborhood of my house at the time when the attempt was made to take me to prison, and that those same agents insisted that the public functionary should execute it.

Be that, as it may, Mr. Editor, nobody respects the prestige of the press more than I do, for I have been one of its members since my early youth. But not for that will I consent by my silence that any one should forge falsehoods in order to excite the public interest to the detriment of my name or the position which I occupy. I am a man who, knowing how to respect the laws and the Commonwealth, also know how to respect myself, and to make myself respected by others. Besides I am accustomed to live in a country, where the residences of citizens are considered sacred, according to the constitution, the law, the press, and the public customs; and I wonder why the case should not be the same in the United States of America.

With regard to the motive of my attempted seizure, it is, "that I propose to fit out an expedition against the dominions of the Queen of Spain," according to the terms of the accusation, I will not at this time say a single word, neither will I explain the errors made by the telegraph in the transmission of the despatches of my honorable friend, Mr. Asta-Buruaga, the Chilian Minister at Washington. For all this the proper time will come before the tribunal of justice, and before the grand jury of public opinion.

Until that time comes, and which I desire may be very

soon, I will only permit myself to say that had I not been born in a country where treason has never been known, and where the people are taught from the cradle to regard betrayal and espionage as an infamy, I could force to accompany me to the tribunal of the United States a brilliant array of numberless prominent men of every public profession in this country—generals, commodores, senators, bankers, diplomatic ministers, journalists, and even the highest functionaries of the republic—who have nobly offered to sustain the cause of the country which I represent, and for which same crime I have been accused.

Nevertheless, it shall not happen, so far as I am concerned ; on the contrary, divesting myself, perhaps voluntarily, of the diplomatic privileges to which I am entitled by law, in order to make its action more expeditious, I will come forward alone to maintain the justice and legality of my proceedings, and then the people of the United States, and the civilized world in general, shall know if the grand principles which were the glory, the power, and the prestige of this country in the old time, are to-day only shadows of the past, or if they may still be seen like a rainbow of hope by free men and free peoples, who may be subjected to the aggressions of crowned usurpers, from the Rio Grande to the Archipelago of Chiloé.

My judgment by these measures will be, not the trial of an individual, but a trial of the present policy, of the oldest and best loved doctrines, of the public sentiment, in fact, of the United States, so strongly uttered every day from the precincts of the humblest country club to the splendid halls of the Capitol of your great republic.

Before concluding, I beg that the journals which have published false or deceptive versions of the event to which this letter refers will have the goodness to reproduce this, for it is the only true one.

I have the honor to be, sir,

Most respectfully,

B. VICUÑA MACKENNA.

In consequence of these proceedings, Mr. Vicuña Mackenna's trial commenced on the 14th of February, before the Circuit Court of the United States, by a preliminary debate, in which Mr. Vicuña Mackenna proved that he was entitled to diplomatic privileges, as claimed in the letter we have just reprinted; after doing which, he declined all immunity, and asked to be tried as a simple citizen.

The following documents, presented and read in court by Mr. Vicuña Mackenna's counsellor, Mr. E. W. Stoughton, refer to the position assumed by the accused.

United States of America,
Southern District of New York, ss. :—

Benjamin Vicuña Mackenna, being duly sworn, says :— That he was born in Santiago, the capital of the State of Chili; that his family have been connected for many years with the public service of that country, his maternal grandfather, General Mackenna having been a member of the earliest executive Government when the country broke the yoke of Spain in 1810, and his paternal grandfather a president of the republic some time after ; that he is a lawyer and an author by profession, having published several historical and political works, and, consequently, a member of many learned societies, both in Europe and South America; that for the last two years he has been a member of the House of Representatives of the Republic of Chili, and Secretary of that body, which position he still retains; that, when the Spanish Government sent a fleet to humiliate and plunder his country, under the most scandalous pretexts, he was requested by the Secretary of State of the republic, Hon. Alvaro Cavarrubias, to come to this country in the capacity of Secretary of the Chilian Legation at Washington, and as confidential agent of the Government, to awaken the public opinion of this country to the righteousness and justice of the cause of Chili, and by this means to increase the feeling of friendship and mutual interest existing between the two countries, which has always (and particularly since the war of the rebellion broke out) been of the most amicable and intimate character, Chili having consented to pay the only claim made by this country upon her treasury, and which before the rebellion the Government had refused to yield for more than thirty years; that he unhesitatingly consented to serve his country in that capacity, and sailed from Valparaiso on the

following day (the 2d of October last) in an English steamer bound to Panamá and thence to this city, where he arrived on the 19th of November; that previous to his departure he had only time to receive a few letters of introduction to this country, having been principally thus favored by the Hon. Thomas H. Nelson, Minister of the
United States in Chili, with whose warm and kind friendship deponent had been honored since his arrival in that
country, this deponent having on several occasions been the
channel of intercourse between Mr. Nelson and the Chilian
Government—that high-minded American representative
being most sincerely esteemed and respected both by
the Government and people of Chili, who looked with
general grief to his removal from office at the moment
when, as senior of the diplomatic body of Chili, he exer-
cised the whole of his influence to bring the Spaniards to
reason. Deponent has had an opportunity of presenting
but a few of Mr. Nelson's letters, among them those addressed to the Hon. Montgomery Blair, Speaker Schuyler
Colfax, Senators Lane, Sumner, and a few others. Among
the letters written by the Hon. Mr. Nelson, and delivered
to deponent on the eve of his departure, was an unsealed
one to the Hon. William H. Seward, Secretary of State,
which, as Mr. Nelson is no longer in office, deponent has
not delivered, but a copy of which he annexes hereto,
marked A, the original being in deponent's possession, and
ready to be produced under the direction of the Court.

Immediately upon deponent's arrival in this country,
as aforesaid, he had an interview with the Chilian Minister, and very soon thereafter delivered several lectures
and speeches in this city, for the purpose of presenting
the war in Chili in its true light of honor, patriotism and
justice against the atrocity of the attack on the part of
Spain; that those demonstrations were made in the presence of thousands of the citizens of New York at the
Cooper Institute, and at various other public places in
this city. That for the same purpose he has made several
publications in pamphlet form, and in the journals of this
city, and has issued a newspaper in the Spanish language,
under the title of *La Vos de la America*, of which several
numbers have been published.

Deponent was in Washington in the month of January
last for several days, and during that time resided in the

house of the Chilian Minister, as a member of his family. Whilst deponent was there, Mr. Seward, Secretary of State, was absent from the country, and Mr. Hunter, who acted as such, was invited to dine with the Chilian Minister, who presented deponent to Mr. Hunter as Secretary of the Chilian Legation, and deponent was also introduced as such, to the President of the United States at a public reception, and, upon other occasions, to Lieutenant-General Grant, Major-General Sherman, and to several other high official persons.

Deponent further says he holds in his possession a document in the Spanish language, in the handwriting of the Chilian Minister, and signed by him, under the seal of the Chilian Embassy at Washington, an exact copy of which document is hereunto annexed, marked B. Deponent now holds and exercises the said office of Secretary of Legation, and is entitled to all the privileges and immunities thereof.

Deponent further says he presents the foregoing facts, and claims his diplomatic privileges because he is advised and believes he ought so to do, in the discharge of his duty to his Government, and not because he has in any manner violated the laws or institutions of the United States, all of which he has ever respected and observed.

BENJ. VICUÑA MACKENNA.

Sworn to before me, this tenth of February, 1866.

EDWARD J. OWEN, Notary Public, N. Y.

LETTER OF HON. THOMAS H. NELSON TO MR. SEWARD.

[A.]   LEGATION OF THE UNITED STATES,
      SANTIAGO DE CHILI, October 1, 1825.

Hon. Wm. H. Seward, Secretary of State, Washington:

MY DEAR SIR:

I have the honor of introducing to you the eminent historian, statesman and patriot, Don Benjamin Vicuña Mackenna, who is on the eve of starting for the United States to represent to our Government and people the condition of affairs in this country. Implicit faith may be given to all that he may say on the subject.

It is scarcely necessary that I should remind you that Mr. Mackenna has ever been our warm and steadfast friend. In the Chilian Congress, in public, and through the press, he has earnestly and eloquently maintained the cause of the Union.

I sincerely hope that he will be received with the consideration due to his eminent character and public services.

Very respectfully,

Your obedient servant,

THOMAS H. NELSON.

LETTER OF THE CHILIAN MINISTER TO MR. V. MACKENNA.

[B.] LEGATION OF CHILI IN THE UNITED STATES OF NORTH AMERICA, WASHINGTON, NOV. 22, 5.

SIR:

The Hon. Secretary of State of Chili informs me that, by order of the Supreme Government, your Excellency has been appointed Secretary of this Legation, with the salary assigned by law, and with the retention of the office of Secretary of the Chamber of Deputies, according to the agreement of that body: the which I have the honor to communicate to your Excellency for your information.

(Signed) F. S. ASTA-BURUAGA.

Explanatory letter of Mr. Asta-Buruaga to Mr. E. W. Stoughton:

[C.] NEW YORK, Feb. 12.

MY DEAR SIR:

As it may prove of interest in the case of Señor Vicuña Mackenna, in which you are counsel, to establish his character, as a man of honor and truth, in its real light, I deem it my duty to state to you that I forwarded to him, at the proper time, the appointment of Secretary of Legation according to instructions which I had received from my Government.

But as Mr. Vicuña Mackenna had not yet been officially

presented to the State Department, he was free to assume or decline that position.

This circumstance explains why the honorable Secretary of State informed the District-Attorney that Mr. Mackenna was not recorded as such Secretary at the State Department; and, at the same time, places in its true light the telegram which I sent to that functionary, stating that Mr. Mackenna *may not be considered as Secretary*, for which purpose I take pleasure in sending you this communication.

I have the honor to to be,

Your obedient servant,

F. S. ASTA-BURUAGA, Chilian Minister.

After reading the above documents, Mr. Stoughton declared in Mr. Vicuña Mackenn's behalf that he was ready to wave, and did wave, all his diplomatic privileges and immunities, and came forward to be tried by the common law of the country.

The Secretary of State, Hon. W. H. Seward, had, nevertheless, refused to grant any diplomatic immunity to the Agent of Chili, as shown in the following telegram and certificate:

TELEGRAM.

WASHINGTON, Feb. 7.

D. S. Dickinson, United States District Attorney.

Benjamin Vicuña Mackenna is not known to this Government as having any diplomatic privileges. You will proceed accordingly.

WILLIAM H. SEWARD.

CERTIFICATE.

UNITED STATES OF AMERICA,
DEPARTMENT OF STATE.

To all to whom these presents shall come greeting:

I certify that it appears, from the records and files of

this Department, that Benjamin Vicuña Mackenna is not now, and never has been, Secretary to the Chilian Legation in the United States, and that he is not and never has been accredited to this Government in any capacity which would entitle him to the privileges and immunities of a diplomatic agent, pursuant to the laws of nations and the Act of Congress in such case provided.

In testimony whereof, I, William H. Seward, Secretary of State of the United States, have hereunto subscribed [LS] my name, and caused the seal of the Department of State to be affixed.

Done at the city of Washington this twelfth day of February, A.D. 1866, and of the Independence of the United States of America the ninetieth.

WILLIAM H. SEWARD.

The trial, after these preliminary discussions, has been postponed to the middle of April, and the Confidential Agent of Chili is at liberty under bail of ten thousand dollars.

What the result of this trial will be time alone will show.

The people of the United States will be called upon to pronounce their verdict in the pending question, and as far as the opinion of its representatives goes, we know its real and deep significance in the account we have published of the meeting of January 6th.

The opinion of the South American countries is not yet known. But the following article, published on February the 21st, by the *Mercantile Chronicle*, of Panamá, an able interpreter of popular feeling among the republics of the Pacific, gives an idea of what will be the feeling exhibited toward the actual policy of the United States in those "sister republics:"

THE ARREST OF THE CHILIAN ENVOY.

From the advices just received from New York, we learn of the arrest of Señor Mackenna, the Special agent of the Republic of Chili to the United States, charged with a breach of the neutrality laws. This action is somewhat startling; but when we consider that Secretary Seward has but recently visited Cuba, and "hobbed and nobbed" with the Captain General, we are not surprised at the action of the State Department even of the free and enlightened United States. Secretary Seward, it is well known, has a *penchant* for "royalty," and that may give us the key, possibly, to many of his anomalous and strange proceedings that damp the ardor of his friends, while they offer to his enemies so fruitful a theme for vituperation. In a land where the "Monroe Doctrine" is supposed to have such a vast hold, Señor Mackenna's breach of the neutrality laws should be scarcely of any moment when placed in the scale against the preservation of republican freedom on this continent. But when the great principle is repudiated in the case of Mexico, it is not to be wondered at that a similar, or even harsher course is adopted toward a distant sister republic like Chili. This arrest was made at the instance of Spaniards and Spanish agents—not United States citizens—and it remains to be seen how the American people receive it.

In contradistinction to the above case, we submit the following: "Within the last fortnight, at the dead of night, in the city of New York, a policeman stopped a suspicious-looking individual in a by-street, driving a wagon loaded with boxes. The driver's answers were unsatisfactory, he was arrested, and the matter brought to the notice of the Superintendent of Police, inasmuch as the load consisted of military accoutrements and clothing. Was this, too, a Chilian enterprise? By no means. *Col. O'Mahony, President of the Irish Republic,* just dropped a 'bit of a note' to the official guardians of the peace, stating that the goods were *his property,* and *presto,* they were released from seizure."

The hope has been for a long time held out to Chili that assistance would be rendered her in her present trying difficulties, and instead thereof, we see her agent arrested like a criminal, while every encouragement and immunity are extended to a lot of hot-headed, crack-brained Irishmen engaged in a mad and hopeless undertaking.

In sober seriousness, what is the meaning of this harsh, unusual proceeding? What does it forebode? "Coming events cast their shadows before," and we look upon the arrest of Señor Mackenna as an evil omen for Chili. But how has this sudden change come about? Is Cuba to be the price paid to the United States by Spain for "lending her a hand" in her present desperate efforts to crush the South American Republics? Who knows !

" There are more things in Heaven and earth, Horatio,
Than are dreamt of in your philosophy !"

www.ingramcontent.com/pod-product-compliance
Lightning Source LLC
Chambersburg PA
CBHW030558040726
47497CB00008B/2774